Writing Resource Guide

A Harcourt Achieve Imprint

www.Rigby.com
1-800-531-5015

Contents

Using the Grammar Lessons and the Writer's Handbook . . iii
Using the Writing Organizers iv
Using the Writer's Craft Lessons v
Writing Assessment Rubric vi
Snapshots of Young Writers viii
Writing Assessment Rubric Form xi
Managing Writing Workshop xii

GRAMMAR LESSONS

Theme 1
Simple and Compound Sentences 1
Simple and Compound Subjects and Predicates 2

Theme 2
Subject–Verb Agreement 3
Sentence Combining 4

Theme 3
Review Sentence Combining 5
Sentence Types 6

Theme 4
Common and Proper Nouns 7
Singular and Plural Nouns 8

Theme 5
Possessive Nouns 9
Subject and Object Nouns 10

Theme 6
Review Nouns 11
Action and Linking Verbs 12

Theme 7
Main and Helping Verbs 13
Past, Present, and Future Verb Tenses 14

Theme 8
Regular and Irregular Verbs 15
Review Verbs 16

Theme 9
Subject and Object Pronouns 17
Possessive Pronouns 18

Theme 10
Singular and Plural Pronouns 19
Review Pronouns 20

Theme 11
Adjectives: Comparative and Superlative 21
Adjectives: Common and Proper 22

Theme 12
Articles 23
Review Adjectives 24

Theme 13
Adverbs 25
Adverbs: Regular and Special Comparison Forms 26

Theme 14
Contractions 27
Prepositions and Prepositional Phrases 28

Theme 15
Conjunctions: Coordinate and Subordinate 29
Independent and Dependent Clauses 30

Theme 16
Homophones 31
Commonly Misused Words 32

WRITING ORGANIZERS
Theme 1: Main Idea and Details Organizer 33
Theme 2: Story Organizer 34
Theme 3: Sequence Organizer 35
Theme 4: Poem Organizer 36
Theme 5: Biography Organizer 37
Theme 6: Problem and Solution Organizer 38
Theme 7: Newspaper Article Organizer 39
Theme 8: Cause and Effect Organizer 40
Theme 9: Report Organizer 41
Theme 10: Sequence Organizer 42
Theme 11: Observation Log Organizer 43
Theme 12: Sequence Organizer 44
Theme 13: Persuasive Essay Organizer 45
Theme 14: Compare and Contrast Organizer 46
Theme 15: Letter Organizer 47
Theme 16: Story Organizer 48

WRITER'S CRAFT LESSONS
Build Suspense in Fiction 49
Include Figurative Language 51
Build Characters 53
Start Strong 55
Build Strong Paragraphs 57
Keep Language Fresh 59
End Effectively 61
Adapt to Purpose and Audience 63

Editing Checklist 65
Writer's Reflection Checklist 66
Writing Traits Checklist 67
Writer's Craft Checklist 68

Using the Grammar Lessons and the Writer's Handbook

Grammar is an essential element in effective writing. Without this fundamental knowledge, students cannot convey their message to an audience.

Lesson Background
- Provides an explanation of the grammar skill.

Teaching the Lesson
- Direct, explicit instruction on the conventions that need to be mastered.
- Refers to the Writer's Handbook for definitions, examples, and grammar rules.

Extending the Lesson
- Reinforces and applies the strategies and techniques targeted during Teaching the Lesson.

On Your Own
- Provides students with an opportunity to practice the skill on their own or with partners.

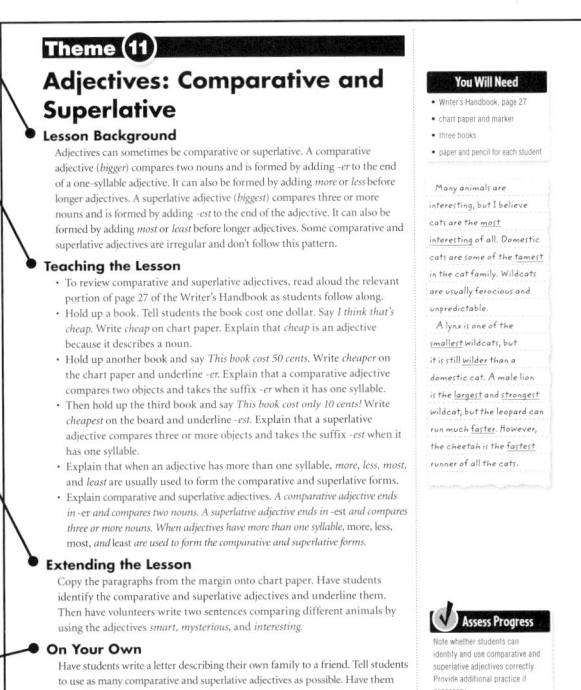

Using the Writer's Handbook

The Writer's Handbook is a valuable reference book for both teachers and students. It can be used with the grammar focus lessons in this guide or to introduce grade-level grammar skills. As students become familiar with grammar, they can use this book as a reference to answer questions about spelling, capitalization, grammar, and usage.

The Writer's Handbook is:

- For teachers to use as they teach focus lessons on grammar, usage, and mechanics during writing instruction.
- For students to use during the Writing Workshop.

Using the Grammar Lessons and the Writer's Handbook

Using the Writing Organizers

The Writing Organizers are reproducible graphic organizers that students use, first in groups and then individually, to develop concepts during prewriting. They are a basic framework for students' compositions. Before students use the Writing Organizers, they have participated in the shared writing process with a teacher using the Writing Transparencies. The Writing Organizer duplicates the graphic organizer used on the Writing Transparency.

Each Writing Workshop focuses on an organizational pattern or a writing form. When featured in explicit instruction, writing forms act as an important supportive frame in which students compose their own ideas. The Writing Organizers provide a hands-on, visual framework to help students organize their ideas and plan their writing.

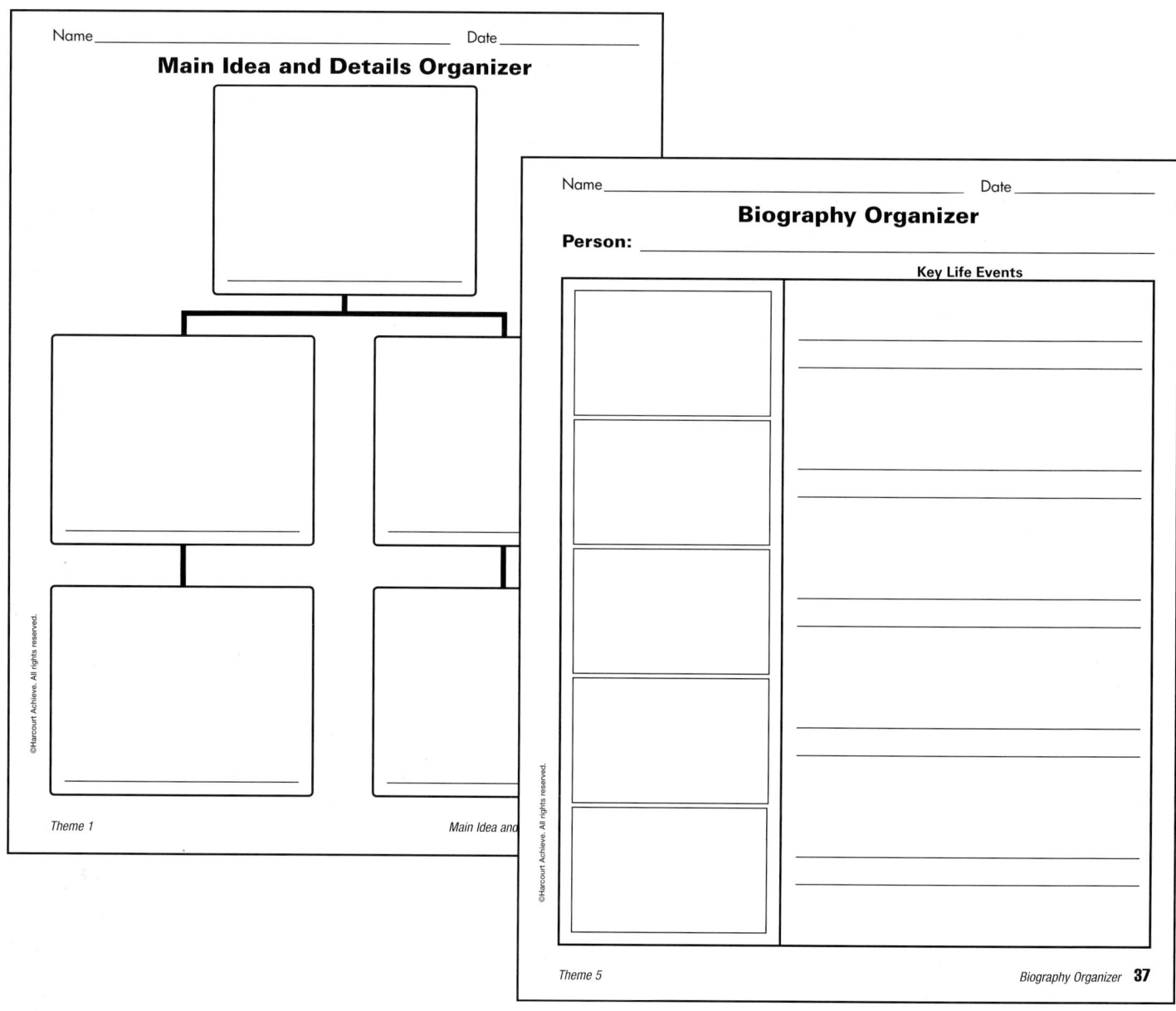

Using the Writer's Craft Lessons

Attention to writer's craft – which covers a host of tools and topics – is an essential way to improve students' writing while reinforcing the notion that the writing process is a craft.

Lesson Background
- Defines the Writer's Craft strategy.

Teaching the Lesson
- Focuses on selections (on the blackline master) that provide a model of the strategy to be addressed in the lesson.

- Guided instruction allows students to analyze and practice the targeted skill in a whole group setting.

Extending the Lesson
- Reinforces skills, strategies, and techniques in small groups or independent writing.

- Focuses on applying the craft skill to students' own work.

On Your Own
- Provides practice in the skill individually or with a partner.

- Encourages the use of the Writer's Notebook.

Whole Group Activity
- Provides a text and an activity for students to practice the craft skill.

- The blackline master can be copied or made into a transparency for instruction.

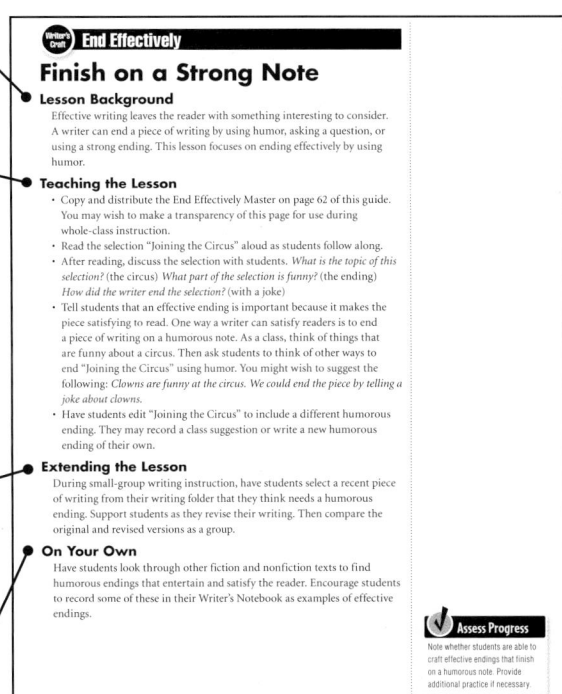

Using the Writer's Craft Lessons   v

Writing Assessment Rubric

The *Literacy by Design* Writing Assessment Rubric contains key behavioral indicators for holistically evaluating the development of young writers. Use the rubric not only to identify the developmental stage of your students but also to plot their future growth, both within and across stages. (See the Writing Assessment Rubric Form on page xi.)

	Experimenting Stage	**Emerging Stage**
Content Ideas and Organization	• Scribbles emulate the look of writing; some may carry meaning. • Simple illustrations represent ideas. • Student shares ideas orally; ideas may lack focus and may vary upon subsequent retellings. • Student may attempt organization by grouping scribbles or illustrations together.	• Illustrations begin to have more detail. • Student orally explains ideas and may elaborate on illustrations or written words and phrases. • Some ideas begin to take shape, but a clear message or storyline may not be present. • Organization continues to develop as student groups similar words and illustrations. • With prompting, student can state audience and purpose.
Language Sentence Fluency, Word Choice, and Voice	• Student shows an awareness that illustrations and written words are different. • Student knows letters and begins to experiment with sound-letter relationships, although some letters may be random. • Illustrations represent common words and generally lack distinguishing features.	• Student demonstrates understanding of one-to-one correspondence between written and spoken words (e.g., student points while reading). • Writing takes the form of simple, common words, phrases, or sentences. • Voice begins to emerge as student adds personal touches to writing and illustrations.
Mechanics Writing Conventions	• Student begins to show an awareness of left-right writing directionality. • Student writes strings of letters and may begin to group letters into words, whether pretend or actual. • Writing is not always legible.	• Clear words emerge, with proper spacing. • Student experiments with uppercase and lowercase letters. • Student begins to group words together into phrases and sentences, arranging them from left to right. • A number of words may be spelled phonetically.
Process Writing Purpose, Process, and Presentation	• Student relies on teacher prompting to draw or "write" about a specific idea. • Student talks about (or explains) work and can be prompted to add to it (e.g., can add more details to a drawing). • Final work may be scattered and disordered on page; illustrations may be labeled.	• Student understands the purpose of and relies upon a small number of text forms (e.g., story, letter). • With guidance, student talks to generate ideas for writing. • Student draws pictures or writes words/phrases about a specific idea. • Student can be prompted to add to the work and make simple corrections. • Final work is mostly legible and more organized; clear use of simple fiction and nonfiction text features (e.g., labels, titles) emerges.

Developing Stage	Proficient Stage	Advanced Stage
• Illustrations, if present, begin to support writing rather than substitute for writing. • A message or storyline is present but may lack a clear beginning or a clear ending. • Some ideas are supported with details but may lack focus. • Ideas show a more formal attempt at organization; some sequencing and use of simple transitions (e.g., words such as *next* or *then*) may be present.	• A clear message or storyline is present, with a serviceable beginning and ending. • Ideas are focused and supported with sufficient details; some details may be weak or off topic. • Ideas are generally well organized; student begins to use more complex transitions to achieve greater passage-level coherence (e.g., transitions that link key content and ideas from sentence to sentence). • Student begins to make choices about ideas and organization to suit audience and purpose.	• A clear message or storyline is present, with an engaging beginning and ending. • Ideas are focused and fully supported with strong, relevant details. • Ideas are well organized; use of transitions and other devices results in writing that is smooth, coherent, and easy to follow. • Student makes strong, effective choices about ideas and organization to suit audience and purpose.
• Simple and compound sentences are used in writing. • Student begins to experiment with different sentence types and syntactical patterns that aid fluency, but overall writing may still be choppy. • Student correctly uses and relies upon a small bank of mostly common words; student may begin to experiment with less common words. • More frequent hints of voice and personality are present, but writing continues to be mostly mechanical.	• More fluent writing emerges through the use of an increasing variety of sentence types and syntactical patterns. • Student correctly uses a large bank of common words; student effectively experiments with new words and begins to choose words more purposefully (e.g., to create images or to have an emotional impact). • Voice continues to develop as student experiments with language.	• All sentence types are present. • Student writes fluently, varying sentence types, sentence beginnings, and grammatical structures. • Student uses an extensive bank of common and less common words correctly; student successfully uses words with precision and purpose. • Voice is expressive, engaging, and appropriate to audience and purpose.
• Sentences have beginning capitalization and ending punctuation; student experiments with other marks (e.g., commas). • Paragraphing begins to emerge. • Spelling is more conventional, especially for high frequency words. • Awareness of usage (i.e., that there are rules to be followed) begins to develop; student experiments with simple usage conventions, but success is variable.	• Student correctly uses all marks of end punctuation; correct use of some other marks is evident, especially in typical situations (e.g., a comma before the conjunction in a compound sentence or a colon to introduce a list). • Student correctly spells most high frequency words and begins to transfer spelling "rules" to lesser-known words. • Writing demonstrates basic understanding of standard grade-level grammar and usage.	• Student correctly and effectively uses standard grade-level punctuation, including more sophisticated marks and usages (e.g., dashes to emphasize key ideas). • Student correctly spells a wide variety of words, both common and uncommon. • Writing demonstrates full and effective control of standard grade-level grammar and usage; overall usage aids reading.
• Student experiments with a variety of text forms and begins to understand how purpose determines form. • Student generates limited prewriting ideas. • With teacher support, draft shows some development but continues to be mostly skeletal. • Student revisits the work but mostly to correct a few line-level errors (e.g., end punctuation and spelling). • Student begins to move more naturally and independently through the writing process. • Final work is generally neat; an increasing variety of fiction and nonfiction text features (e.g., titles, headings, charts, captions) is present, but features may be more for show than for support of message.	• Student demonstrates increasing control over a variety of text forms and can choose form to suit purpose. • Student generates sufficient prewriting ideas. • Draft shows good development of prewriting, including effective attempts at focusing, organizing, and elaborating ideas. • Student revisits the work not only to correct errors but also to address some passage-level issues (e.g., clarity of message, sufficiency of details); student may use supporting resources (e.g., dictionary, grammar book). • Sense that the process is purposeful begins to emerge. • Final work is neat; use of various fiction and nonfiction text features tends to support and clarify meaning.	• Student effectively controls a variety of text forms and can choose form to suit purpose. • Student uses prewriting ideas as a plan that is both general and flexible. • Draft shows strong development of prewriting and may effectively depart from prewriting as a signal of the student's overall writing maturity. • Student revisits the work not only to correct errors but also to address key passage-level issues. • Overall, student shows investment in the craft of writing and moves through the stages smoothly and recursively. • Final work is neat; effective use of fiction and nonfiction text features results in a polish that strengthens the student's overall message.

Snapshots of Young Writers

Writing samples, or anchor papers, provide powerful snapshots of writing development—snapshots key to understanding students' control over written language and to determining subsequent paths of instruction. The following writing samples represent each of the five stages of development in the *Literacy by Design* Writing Assessment Rubric. The samples for each stage are preceded by a brief summary of key behavioral indicators for that stage.

Experimenting Stage

- Writing is mostly an attempt to emulate adult writing.
- It includes single letters, letter strings, and simple illustrations.
- Writing attempts to be communicative, but most letters and letter strings do not carry consistent meaning.

Nour

Mireya

Emerging Stage

- Writing shows an understanding that spoken words can be written down and read by others.
- It includes the use of content-bearing words, phrases, and short sentences.
- Writing may demonstrate left-right directionality and experimentation with capital letters and end marks.
- It includes many words spelled phonetically.

Ricky

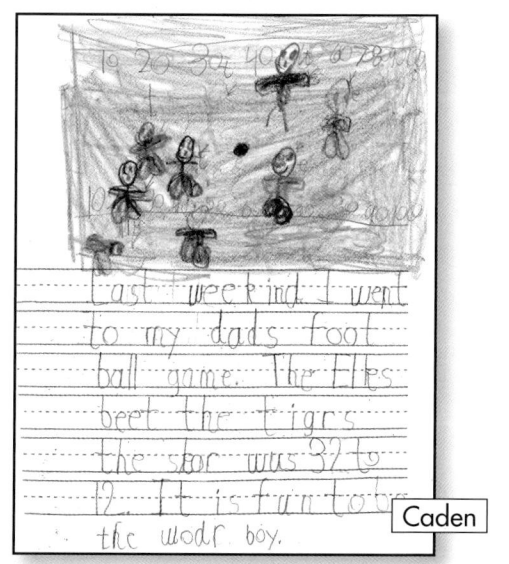
Caden

viii   Snapshots of Young Writers

Developing Stage
- Writing exhibits growing control over writing conventions, including more conventional spelling, punctuation, and grammar.
- Writing carries a simple message supported by some details.
- Sentence structure is mostly formulaic and mechanical.
- It includes a limited number of text forms.

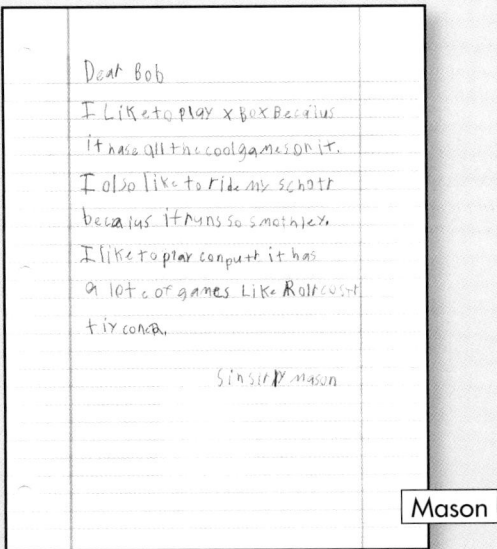
Mason

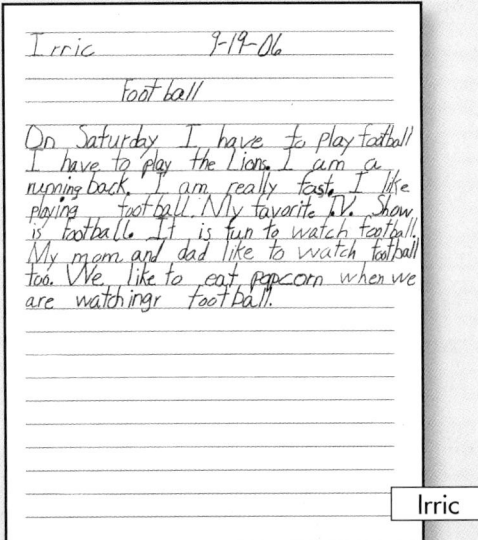
Irric

Proficient Stage
- Writing includes a clear, focused message supported by sufficient details.
- It exhibits most grade-level conventions.
- Writing includes a variety of sentence structures.
- It shows a growing awareness of audience and purpose.
- It demonstrates control over a variety of text forms.

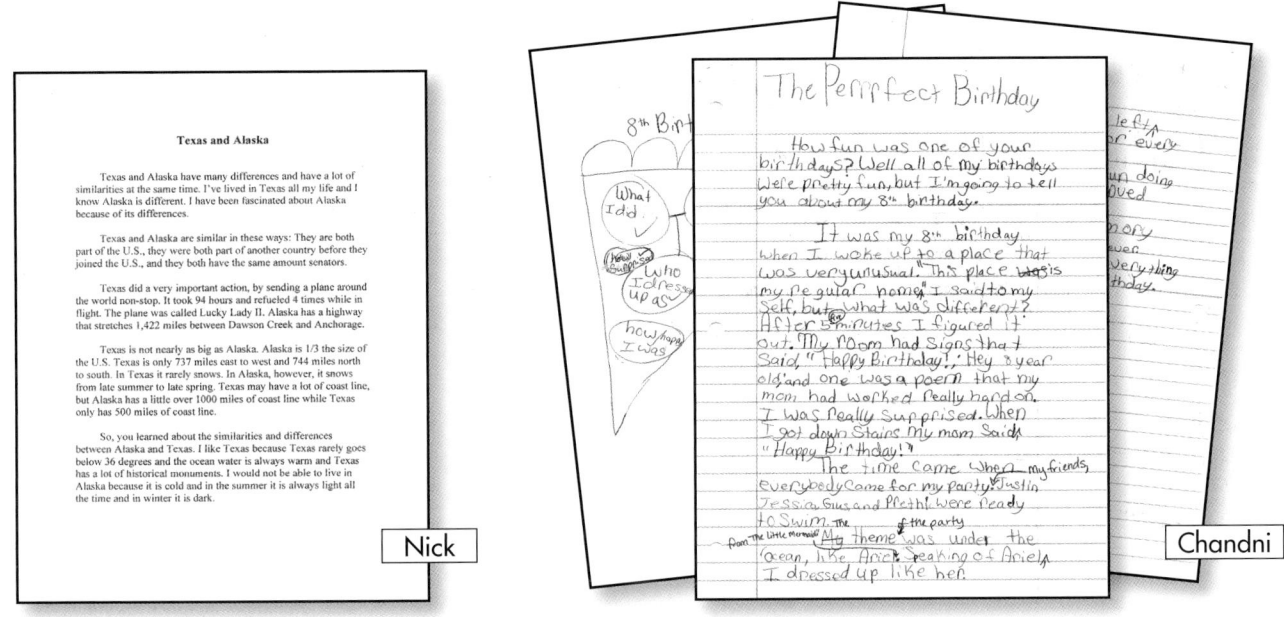
Nick

Chandni

Snapshots of Young Writers   **ix**

Advanced Stage

- Writing demonstrates mastery of conventions and purposeful variety of sentence structures.
- It includes a strong, focused message that is fully supported and engaging in presentation.
- Writing exhibits a clear understanding of audience and purpose.
- It shows effective use of word choice, voice, details, and text form.

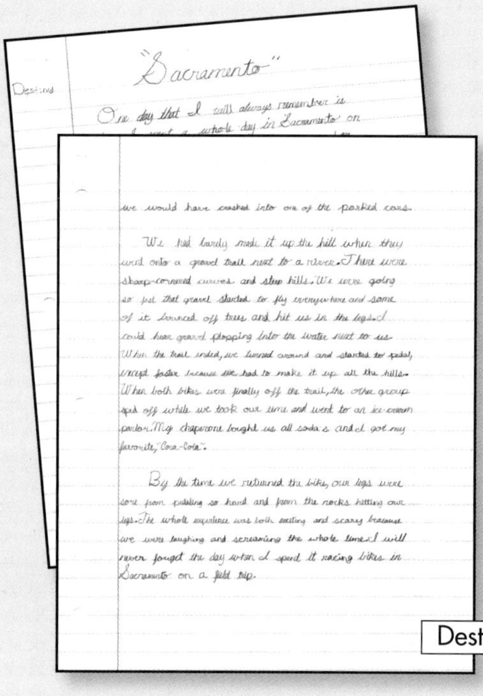

[Destiny — handwritten essay "Sacramento"]

[Brandon — typed essay on I. M. Pei]

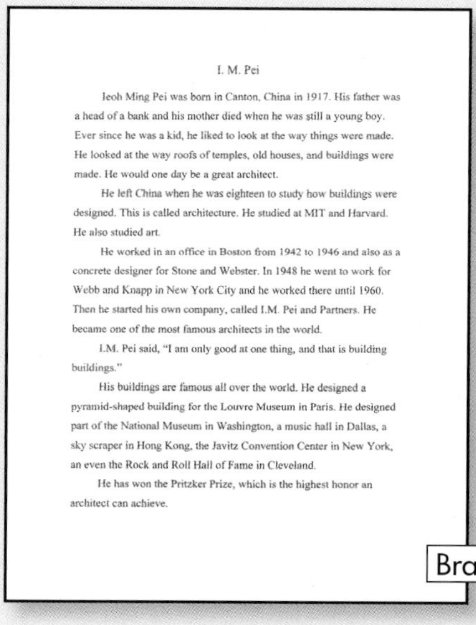

I. M. Pei

Ieoh Ming Pei was born in Canton, China in 1917. His father was a head of a bank and his mother died when he was still a young boy. Ever since he was a kid, he liked to look at the way things were made. He looked at the way roofs of temples, old houses, and buildings were made. He would one day be a great architect.

He left China when he was eighteen to study how buildings were designed. This is called architecture. He studied at MIT and Harvard. He also studied art.

He worked in an office in Boston from 1942 to 1946 and also as a concrete designer for Stone and Webster. In 1948 he went to work for Webb and Knapp in New York City and he worked there until 1960. Then he started his own company, called I.M. Pei and Partners. He became one of the most famous architects in the world.

I.M. Pei said, "I am only good at one thing, and that is building buildings."

His buildings are famous all over the world. He designed a pyramid-shaped building for the Louvre Museum in Paris. He designed part of the National Museum in Washington, a music hall in Dallas, a sky scraper in Hong Kong, the Javitz Convention Center in New York, an even the Rock and Roll Hall of Fame in Cleveland.

He has won the Pritzker Prize, which is the highest honor an architect can achieve.

Writing Stages According to Grade Level

	Experimenting Stage	Emerging Stage	Developing Stage	Proficient Stage	Advanced Stage
Grade K	▬▬▬▬▬				
Grade 1		▬▬▬▬▬			
Grade 2		▬▬▬▬▬			
Grade 3			▬▬▬▬▬		
Grade 4				▬▬▬	
Grade 5				▬▬▬▬▬	

Snapshots of Young Writers

Writing Assessment Rubric Form

Student's Name _____ **Date** _____

(1)
- Based on an initial review of a representative sampling of student work, identify the student's most likely stage of development. Locate that stage on the rubric and then review the behavioral indicators for each of the four instructional categories: Content, Language, Mechanics, and Process.
- If the indicators for a particular category mostly describe the student's work, check the appropriate box.
- The student is considered to be in a particular stage if at least three category boxes in that stage have been checked. If fewer than three boxes are checked, the student is considered to be in the previous stage.

	Experimenting	Emerging	Developing	Proficient	Advanced
Content Ideas and Organization	☐	☐	☐	☐	☐
Language Sentence Fluency, Word Choice, and Voice	☐	☐	☐	☐	☐
Mechanics Writing Conventions	☐	☐	☐	☐	☐
Process Writing Purpose, Process, and Presentation	☐	☐	☐	☐	☐

Stage _____

(2)
- Note observations about key strengths and weaknesses.
- Tie observations to specific strategies to be used in future instruction.

Observations	Notes for Future Instruction
Strengths	➡
Growth Areas	➡

* It is recommended that you use the *Literacy by Design* Writing Assessment Rubric to evaluate a sampling of each student's writing at least three times a year.

Managing Writing Workshop

Independent Writing at the Core
Similar to reading workshop, writing workshop is the time when a teacher works with a small group of students to differentiate writing instruction. Other students are engaged in writing independently, whether that means generating ideas, writing a draft, or revising their writing.

Students learn to write with practice. They need ample classroom time to explore ideas and refine their writing skills. Independent writing allows students to apply the strategies and skills they are learning in whole class and small group instruction.

A key difference between small group writing and small group reading is that student writers are typically working on the same piece as they move from the group to independent work. In fact, a writer might continue work on the same writing piece over several small group sessions, continuing to work on the piece between sessions in independent writing as well. Having the two activities occur simultaneously in the same workshop emphasizes the connection between small group and independent writing.

Making Independent Writing Successful
- **Conference regularly with writers.** Meet with students to ensure they use their Writer's Notebook or other resources when recording ideas and finding writing topics (See *Comprehensive Teacher's Guide*, Writing Conference Form, page A23).

- **Provide a focus for independent writing.** Choose a writing form, organizational pattern, process, or trait that is taught in the theme to serve as a focus for students during independent writing.

- **Offer prompts when writers get stuck.** The best source for writing ideas is a student's Writer's Notebook, but occasionally students just get stuck. Provide specific prompts related to the theme's instructional focus that can be used when students are having difficulty identifying a topic for their writing.

Setting Up Writing Workshop
In a successful writing workshop, students understand and embrace the opportunity to explore ideas and mold those ideas into text. Planning requires setting up materials and creating an environment in which students can manage their independent writing time effectively.

Create a Space for a Successful Writing Workshop
- Designated place for students to keep their **writing folders** and **Writer's Notebooks**
- **Reference area** with dictionaries, encyclopedias, and thesauruses
- **Writing center** with magazines and other visual materials to spark ideas
- Wall space to display **shared** and **interactive writing pieces**
- Copies of **graphic organizers** to capture and organize writing ideas (see pages 33–48)

Theme 1

Simple and Compound Sentences

Lesson Background
A simple sentence has only one independent clause and expresses one complete thought. A compound sentence consists of two or more simple sentences that are linked by a comma and a conjunction.

Teaching the Lesson
- To review simple and compound sentences, read aloud the relevant portion of page 35 of the Writer's Handbook as students follow along.
- Tape the sentence strips to the board. Ask students to identify the subject(s) and predicate(s) in each sentence. Circle the subjects and underline the predicates of each sentence. Ask students how many complete thoughts are in each sentence. Explain that the first two sentences are simple sentences. The third sentence is compound. It combines the first two sentences by adding a comma and the connecting word *and*.
- Write the following sentence on chart paper: *Helena liked children, but she did not have time to babysit.* Say *This is a compound sentence because there is one complete thought before and after the connecting word.* Have a volunteer underline the simple sentences.
- Explain simple and compound sentences. *A simple sentence expresses one complete thought. A compound sentence is two simple sentences joined by a comma and a connecting word.*

Extending the Lesson
Copy the sentences from the margin onto chart paper. Tape the index cards with the connecting words and commas in random order next to the chart. Have students join each pair of simple sentences by adding a comma and the proper connecting word.

On Your Own
Have students write a paragraph explaining their favorite thing to do. Tell them to use at least two simple sentences and two compound sentences.

You Will Need
- Writer's Handbook, page 35
- sentence strips with the following sentences written on them:
  I wore a coat and scarf.
  My brother and I went sledding.
  I wore a coat and scarf, and my brother and I went sledding.
- tape
- chart paper and marker
- index cards with the following words written on them: *and, but, so*
- three index cards with commas
- paper and pencil for each student

---

1. She forgot her homework. She remembered her lunch. [but]
2. The teacher took her class to the library. Her class picked out new books. [and]
3. The football player forgot to wear his helmet. He got hurt. [so]

 **Assess Progress**

Note whether students are able to identify and form simple and compound sentences. Provide additional practice if necessary.

Theme 1

Simple and Compound Subjects and Predicates

Lesson Background

The simple subject of a sentence is the noun or pronoun that performs the action. The simple predicate of a sentence is the verb. A sentence has a compound subject if more than one simple subject performs the same action. A sentence has a compound predicate if there are two or more simple predicates.

Teaching the Lesson

- To review simple and compound subjects and predicates, read aloud the relevant portion of page 34 of the Writer's Handbook as students follow along.
- Have three volunteers come to the front of the room. Have one sit and the others stand. Write the following on chart paper: [Student's name] *is sitting.* [Student's name] *and* [student's name] *are standing.* Explain that the student's name in the first sentence is the simple subject. The sentence has only one subject. The subject in the second sentence is compound. The sentence has more than one simple subject performing an action.
- Ask students to write a sentence about one food they enjoy eating. Then ask them to write a sentence about two things they do after school. Ask a volunteer to read his or her sentences aloud. Explain that the first sentence has a simple predicate and the second has a compound predicate.
- Explain simple and compound subjects and predicates. *A simple subject is the noun that performs the action, and the simple predicate is the verb. Compound subjects have more than one simple subject, and compound predicates have more than one simple predicate.*

Extending the Lesson

Copy the sentences in the margin onto chart paper. Have students rewrite each sentence, following the instructions provided.

On Your Own

Have students copy examples of sentences from books in the classroom. Ask them to circle the simple subjects and underline the simple predicates. Tell them to label the subjects and predicates as either simple or compound.

You Will Need

- Writer's Handbook, page 34
- chart paper and marker
- paper and pencil for each student
- books for examples of simple and compound subjects and predicates

---

1. Eva went to the movies. (Make the subject compound.)
2. The teachers and parents met with the principal. (Make the subject simple.)
3. José and his father hiked and went fishing. (Make the predicate simple.)
4. Sung Yee went to the library. (Make the predicate compound.)
5. Jamie cleaned the house. (Make both the subject and the predicate compound.)
6. Max and his brother work at the grocery store and deliver newspapers. (Make both the subject and the predicate simple.)

 **Assess Progress**

Note whether students can identify and create simple and compound subjects and predicates. Provide additional practice if necessary.

Theme 2
Subject-Verb Agreement

Lesson Background
In all sentences, the subjects and verbs must agree. When the subject of a sentence is singular, the verb must also be singular. When the subject of a sentence is plural, the verb must also be plural.

Teaching the Lesson
- To review subject and verb agreement, read aloud the relevant portion of page 24 of the Writer's Handbook as students follow along.
- On chart paper write *Diego takes the bus to school.* Underline *Diego* and circle *takes*. Point out that *Diego* is a singular subject (he is only one person) and *takes* is a singular verb. (It is used for only one person.) Then write *The students take the bus to school.* Ask a volunteer to underline the subject and circle the verb in the new sentence. Ask students what has changed about the subject and verb in the second sentence. (Both the subject and verb are plural in the second sentence.)
- Write the following sentences on chart paper: *My brother and I walk my dog in the park. He walks the dog in the park.* Have students determine whether the subjects are plural or singular. (plural, singular)
- Explain subject and verb agreement. *When the subject of a sentence is singular, the verb should also be singular. When the subject of a sentence is plural, the verb should also be plural.*

Extending the Lesson
Copy the sentences from the margin onto chart paper. Have students choose the subject or verb that makes each sentence correct.

On Your Own
Have students write four sentences that are missing a singular or plural verb. Then have students trade papers with a partner and fill in the missing verbs.

You Will Need
- Writer's Handbook, page 24
- chart paper and marker
- paper and pencil for each student

---

1. Rory (shoot/shoots) baskets after school.
2. (He/They) never go to the old playground anymore.
3. The fifth grade teachers (take/takes) the entire class on a field trip every year.
4. (The principal/The principal and assistant principal) schedules all the assemblies for the afternoons.
5. (That library/Those libraries) has more than 10,000 books.
6. I (like/likes) puzzles and solving problems, so I (plan/plans) to be a scientist or a detective in the future.

 **Assess Progress**

Note whether students understand subject-verb agreement. Provide additional practice if necessary.

Theme 2

Sentence Combining

Lesson Background

When students use a lot of short sentences, the writing may be choppy and rough. There are several ways to avoid this problem. One way is to combine sentence fragments to create complete sentences. Students can also combine sentences using compound subjects or predicates. Another way is to join two simple sentences with a conjunction to create a compound sentence.

Teaching the Lesson

- To introduce sentence combining and sentence fragments, read aloud the relevant portions of pages 35–36 and 45–46 of the Writer's Handbook as students follow along.
- Tape the sentence strips to the board. Ask students why the first strip is not a sentence. (It doesn't express a complete thought.) Work with students to combine the sentence strips into one complete sentence. (*When I listen to music, I like to tap my foot* or *I like to tap my foot when I listen to music.*)
- Write the following sentences on chart paper: *Kareem plays drums. Carl plays drums.* Ask students what is repeated in both sentences. Circle the words *plays drums* in each sentence. Write *Kareem and Carl play drums.* Underline *play.* Remind students that the sentence needs a plural verb because there are two subjects.
- Write on chart paper *Anthony plays guitar. Anthony writes songs.* Circle *Anthony* in both sentences. Explain that you can combine predicates when the subject is the same. Write *Anthony plays guitar and writes songs.*
- Write on chart paper *Ai plays golf. Bree and Marc don't like sports.* Explain that sentences can also be combined by adding a comma and a conjunction. Write *Ai plays golf, but Bree and Marc don't like sports.*
- Explain how to combine sentences. *You can combine short, repetitive sentences by creating compound subjects or predicates or by creating compound sentences. Sentence fragments can be combined with other fragments or sentences to create complete sentences.*

Extending the Lesson

Copy the sentences in the margin onto chart paper. Have students combine the short sentences and sentence fragments to make longer sentences.

On Your Own

Have students write a paragraph about the kinds of music they like. Have pairs exchange papers and edit each other's paragraph, combining any sentence fragments and short, repetitive sentences.

You Will Need

- Writer's Handbook, pages 35–36 and 45–46
- chart paper and marker
- sentence strips with the following written on them: *When I listen to music. I like to tap my foot.*
- tape
- paper and pencil for each student

---

1. Although he doesn't like it. Evan must practice hitting the ball.
2. David plays the saxophone. Harry plays the saxophone.
3. Eva plays the flute. Eva plays the trumpet.
4. Yun Hee used to swim on the swim team. She runs track now.
5. Rachel plays piano. She also sings in the choir. She also runs on the track team.
6. When my grandma bakes a blueberry pie. The whole house smells amazing.

 **Assess Progress**

Note whether students are able to combine short, repetitive sentences and combine sentence fragments to create complete sentences. Provide additional practice if necessary.

Theme 3

Review Sentence Combining

Lesson Background

Short, repetitive sentences with redundant information can be combined into longer, smoother sentences. One way to combine sentences is by creating compound subjects or compound predicates. Another way is by joining two sentences with a conjunction to make a compound sentence. Sentence fragments must be rewritten as complete sentences.

Teaching the Lesson

- To review sentence combining and sentence fragments, read aloud the relevant portions of pages 35–36 and 45–46 of the Writer's Handbook as students follow along.
- Write the following fragment and sentence on chart paper: *Because she plays basketball and soccer. Andrea gets to run around every day after school.* Ask students whether both of these are sentences. (No, the first one is a fragment.) Work with students to combine the fragment and sentence.
- Write these sentences on chart paper: *Andy was late. His sister was late. Andy missed the bus. His sister missed the bus.* Ask students what is wrong with the sentences. (They are repetitious.) Ask students to combine the sentences. (*Andy and his sister were late, so they missed the bus.*) Explain that this sentence is a compound sentence with a compound subject.
- Tape the sentence strips to the board. Have students rewrite the sentences and fragment by combining. (*The old house was empty and run-down. Although it was for sale, no one wanted to live there or even ring the doorbell.*)
- Explain the purpose of combining sentences. *Combining sentences makes them less repetitive and more interesting to read. One way to combine sentences is to create compound subjects and predicates. Another way is to join simple sentences to form a compound sentence. Fragments are not complete sentences, so they must be combined with other fragments or sentences.*

Extending the Lesson

Copy the paragraph from the margin onto chart paper. Have students note sentences with repetitive subjects or predicates. Then have students rewrite the paragraph, combining sentences to make them less repetitive and to eliminate any fragments.

On Your Own

Have students write a few sentences about a favorite place. Then have them exchange papers and combine sentences as needed to make the sentences less repetitive and eliminate any fragments.

You Will Need
- Writer's Handbook, pages 35–36 and 45–46
- chart paper and marker
- sentence strips with the following sentences written on them:
  The old house was empty.
  The old house was run-down.
  Although it was for sale.
  No one wanted to live there.
  No one even wanted to ring the doorbell.
- tape
- paper and pencil for each student

Every Thursday I go to my grandma's house. Because my mother works late on Thursdays. My grandma's house is cluttered. She has lots of photographs. She owns many books, too. It's very messy. It's also cozy. I like to look at the old family photos. My grandma also likes to look at old family photos. I like to learn about family history.

 **Assess Progress**

Note whether students are able to combine sentences. Provide additional practice if necessary.

Theme 3

Sentence Types

Lesson Background

Sentences can have different purposes. A declarative sentence makes a statement. An interrogative sentence asks a question. An imperative sentence gives a command. An exclamatory sentence shows strong emotion.

Teaching the Lesson

- To review sentence types, read aloud the relevant portions of pages 35–36 of the Writer's Handbook as students follow along.
- Tape the sentence strips to the board. Have a volunteer read the first sentence aloud. Ask students what punctuation mark will complete the sentence. Write a question mark. Tell students that questions are also called interrogative sentences.
- Have a volunteer read the second sentence aloud in a calm, quiet voice. Ask students what punctuation mark will complete the sentence. Add a period. Have the volunteer reread the sentence aloud, this time in a loud, angry voice. Ask students what punctuation mark will complete the sentence now. Add an exclamation point. Explain that a sentence that is a command is called an imperative sentence. It can take either a period or an exclamation point, depending on how forceful the command is.
- Have a volunteer read the third sentence aloud. Ask students to determine the correct punctuation mark and add a period. Explain to students that statements are also called declarative sentences.
- Have a volunteer read the fourth sentence aloud. Ask students to determine the correct punctuation mark. Add an exclamation point. Explain that sentences that express strong emotion and end with an exclamation point are called exclamatory sentences.
- Explain the four types of sentences. *Declarative sentences are statements, interrogative sentences are questions, imperative sentences are commands, and exclamatory sentences show strong feeling.*

Extending the Lesson

Copy the paragraph from the margin onto chart paper. Have volunteers punctuate the paragraph correctly and identify the sentence types.

On Your Own

Have each student look through books in the classroom and find a paragraph with more than one type of sentence. Have students copy the paragraph without punctuation, exchange papers with a partner, and add the correct punctuation with a colored pencil.

You Will Need

- Writer's Handbook, pages 35–36
- sentence strips with the following sentences written on them:
  Where are we going
  Get in the car
  We're driving to the science museum
  The dinosaur exhibit is the absolute best
- tape
- chart paper and marker
- paper, pencil, and colored pencil for each student
- books for example sentences

It was awful ___ Gabriela had forgotten her mother's birthday ___ "What should I do ___" she asked. She had never forgotten her mother's birthday before ___ She walked home from school sadly ___ She passed some flowers growing by the side of the road ___ "Look at that ___" she cried. Beautiful tiger lilies were growing next to a tree ___ She picked the flowers ___ When she got home, she put the flowers in a vase and gave them to her mother ___

 Assess Progress

Note whether students can identify declarative, interrogative, imperative, and exclamatory sentences. Provide additional practice if necessary.

Theme 4

Common and Proper Nouns

Lesson Background
A noun names a person, place, thing, or idea. Common nouns are general and start with a lowercase letter. Proper nouns are specific and start with a capital letter. Proper nouns include people's names, titles, days, months, holidays, organizations, religions, nationalities, and languages.

Teaching the Lesson
- To review common and proper nouns, read aloud the relevant portions of pages 4–7 and 20 of the Writer's Handbook as students follow along.
- Draw a T-chart on chart paper. On the left side, list these nouns: *Ms. Jones, Chinese, Monday, Brazilians.* On the right side, list these nouns: *teacher, language, day of the week, people.* Ask students to discuss the similarities and differences between the two lists. Emphasize that the left side contains proper nouns that name specific things, while the right side contains common nouns that name general things. Point out the initial capital letter in all the proper nouns.
- Label the left side of the chart *Proper Nouns* and the right side *Common Nouns*. Have students suggest more proper and common nouns to add to the list.
- Explain the difference between proper and common nouns. *Proper nouns are specific and begin with a capital letter. Common nouns are general and begin with a lowercase letter.*

Extending the Lesson
Copy the paragraph from the margin onto chart paper. Have students capitalize all the proper nouns and circle the common nouns.

On Your Own
Have students list at least two proper nouns for each category listed in the "Proper Nouns" list in the margin. Encourage early finishers to add more examples to their lists.

You Will Need
- Writer's Handbook, pages 4–7 and 20
- chart paper and marker
- paper and pencil for each student

---

may 5 is a holiday in mexico. In 1862, troops in mexico defeated the french. The army was led by general ignacio zaragoza. Across mexico, people commemorate the battle of pueblo on may 5 each year. People in several cities in the united states, such as los angeles and denver, celebrate the holiday.

Proper Nouns
a city
a country
a day of the week
a holiday
a month
a nationality
a person's name
a person's title

✓ Assess Progress

Note whether students can distinguish between common and proper nouns as well as capitalize proper nouns correctly. Provide additional practice if necessary.

Theme 4

Singular and Plural Nouns

Lesson Background
A noun names a person, place, thing, or idea. Singular nouns name one person, place, thing, or idea, while plural nouns name more than one. Plural nouns are usually formed by adding -s or -es to the singular form. Some nouns have irregular plural forms that must be memorized.

Teaching the Lesson
- To introduce singular and plural nouns, read aloud the relevant portion of page 20 of the Writer's Handbook as students follow along.
- Tape the first two sentence strips to the board. Note that *acrobat* is singular while *acrobats* is plural and ends in -s.
- Tape the next two sentence strips to the board. Explain to students that when a singular noun ends in -ch, -s, -sh, or -x, you form its plural by adding -es. Note that you can hear the extra syllable when you say the plural form of these words.
- Tape the last sentence strip to the board. Explain to students that when a noun ends in a consonant plus -y, you usually change the -y to an -i and add -es to form the plural. When the noun ends in a vowel plus -y, the plural form ends with an -s.
- Explain that some nouns are irregular and don't follow the patterns. Write *one man, two men*. Then write *one woman, two ____*. Have students identify the plural. Repeat with *one person, two ____*.
- Explain the difference between singular and plural nouns and the conventions of forming plurals. *A singular noun names one person, place, thing, or idea. A plural noun names more than one person, place, thing, or idea. Most nouns take an -s or -es at the end of the word when they are plural, but other nouns have special rules for forming plurals.*

Extending the Lesson
Copy the paragraph and word bank from the margin onto chart paper. Have students complete the paragraph using the correct plural form of each word from the word bank.

On Your Own
Have students create a T-chart. Tell them to label one side *Singular* and the other *Plural*. Ask them to think of ten nouns and write the singular and plural forms of each noun in the correct columns.

You Will Need
- Writer's Handbook, page 20
- chart paper and marker
- sentence strips with the following sentences written on them:
  1. One <u>acrobat</u> swung on the trapeze.
  2. Then another joined her, and there were two <u>acrobats</u>.
  3. We need two <u>boxes</u> of <u>matches</u>.
  4. While I was washing <u>dishes</u>, I accidentally broke two <u>glasses</u>.
  5. The <u>boys</u> decided that <u>babies</u> were noisy but cute.
- tape
- paper and pencil for each student

I made four ____ by the wishing well. I took four ____ and dropped them in the water. First I wished for two ____ to ride and two new ____ to play with. But these wishes were too greedy. Then I wished my ____ would all be happy. Finally I wished that all the ____ around the world would be happy and safe.

WORD BANK
penny	child	friend
pony	toy	wish

Assess Progress
Note whether students can differentiate between singular and plural nouns. Provide additional practice if necessary.

Theme 5
Possessive Nouns

Lesson Background
A possessive noun shows to whom or to what an object belongs. An apostrophe and -s are used to indicate a singular possessive noun. A plural possessive noun is indicated by an apostrophe placed after the -s at the end of the word. Irregular nouns that are possessive and end in a letter other than -s should have an apostrophe plus an -s at the end of the noun.

Teaching the Lesson
- To review possessive nouns, read aloud the relevant portions of pages 19 and 21 of the Writer's Handbook as students follow along.
- Tape the sentence strips to the board. Ask volunteers to underline the possessive nouns. Then have students circle the noun each possessive noun describes. Review the possessive noun in each sentence and ask students whether the noun is singular (one), plural (more than one), or shared. Note that shared possessives, like *Connor and Patrick's*, need only one apostrophe and -s placed after the second noun.
- Write these phrases on chart paper: *Jupiter _____ spot, Mercury _____ orbit, Neptune and Saturn _____ rings, Earth _____ atmosphere, Planets _____ surfaces.* Have students form the correct possessive noun for each.
- Write the following sentences on chart paper. *The boys choir sings at the school festival. The womens baseball team has a record of six wins and two losses.* Ask students where to put the apostrophe in each of the underlined plural possessive nouns. (boys', women's) Explain that plural nouns that end in -s get an apostrophe at the end of the word, but plural nouns that end in other letters need an apostrophe and then an -s.
- Explain how to create possessive nouns. *Possessive nouns show ownership. An apostrophe and an -s are usually used to form a possessive noun. Shared possessives need only one apostrophe and -s. Plural possessives that end in -s need only an apostrophe. Irregular plural possessives need an apostrophe and an -s.*

Extending the Lesson
Copy the sentences in the margin onto chart paper. Have students fill in the blanks with the correct possessive noun form.

On Your Own
Collect five classroom items from volunteers. Hold up the items in front of the students and describe who owns each item. Have students write a few sentences describing the items. Ask students to use at least five possessive nouns.

You Will Need
- Writer's Handbook, pages 19 and 21
- chart paper and marker
- sentence strips with the following written on them:
  Everyone wanted to pet Yolanda's dog.
  Connor and Patrick's room needed to be cleaned.
  The monkeys' cages are near the entrance.
- tape
- paper and pencil for each student
- five classroom items from different students

1. _____ favorite tree is the maple tree. (Paolo) [Paolo's]
2. The _____ meeting was held in the cafeteria. (teachers) [teachers']
3. _____ karate class is at the youth center. (Gloria) [Gloria's]
4. That is _____ grandmother. (Darnell and Keisha) [Darnell and Keisha's]
5. The _____ whiskers are long. (cat) [cat's]
6. The _____ story time is at 2 p.m. (library) [library's]

 Assess Progress

Note whether students can identify and form possessive nouns. Provide additional practice if necessary.

Theme 5

Subject and Object Nouns

Lesson Background

A noun is a person, place, thing, or idea. A subject noun is the noun that performs the action in a sentence. An object noun receives the action of the verb or is part of a prepositional phrase. An object noun can be direct or indirect.

Teaching the Lesson

- To introduce subject and object nouns, read aloud the relevant portion of page 21 of the Writer's Handbook as students follow along.
- Write the following sentence on chart paper: *Tess rode a huge roller coaster.* Ask students who performed the action in the sentence. Underline *Tess* and write *subject* above the word. Explain that a subject noun performs the action in this sentence. Ask students what Tess rode. Underline *roller coaster* and write *object* above the words. Explain that an object noun receives the action of a verb and usually follows it.
- Tape the first sentence strip to the chart paper. Ask a volunteer to underline each noun. Then identify and label the nouns as subject or object nouns. (*Yuki*, subject; *basketball*, object)
- Tape the second sentence strip to the chart paper and repeat the underlining and labeling procedure. Point out that the sentence has two objects. Say *The word* bike *is the direct object because it receives the action of the verb.* Sister *is the indirect object because the action of the sentence is being done for her.*
- Tape the third strip to the chart paper and repeat the underlining and labeling procedure. Tell students that the word *store* is an object noun because it is the object of a prepositional phrase.
- Explain to students the difference between subject and object nouns. *A subject noun performs the action in a sentence. An object noun receives the action of the verb or is the object of a prepositional phrase. A direct object receives the action of the verb in a sentence. An indirect object names the person or thing to or for whom the subject does the action.*

Extending the Lesson

Copy the sentences from the margin onto chart paper. Have students circle subject nouns in blue and object nouns in red.

On Your Own

Have students write a short paragraph about their favorite book or movie. Tell them to use at least two pairs of subject and object nouns. Then have them switch papers with a partner and label the nouns as either subjects or objects.

You Will Need

- Writer's Handbook, page 21
- chart paper and marker
- sentence strips with the following sentences written on them:
  Yuki dribbled a basketball.
  Dennis loaned his sister his ten-speed bike.
  Suri brought a pie from her store.
- tape
- paper, pencil, and colored pencils (red and blue) for each student

---

1. Greg is holding a pen. [Greg, subject; pen, object]
2. Leila studied chemistry. [Leila, subject; chemistry, object]
3. The boy ate some toast. [boy, subject; toast, object]
4. Robert read a book to Susie. [Robert, subject; book, Susie, objects]
5. The sun is shining on my head. [sun, subject; head, object]

 Assess Progress

Note whether students can differentiate between subject and object nouns. Provide additional practice if necessary.

---

10 Theme 5   *Subject and Object Nouns*

Theme 6

Review Nouns

Lesson Background

A noun is a person, place, thing, or idea. Students have learned about common and proper nouns, singular and plural nouns, subject and object nouns, and possessive nouns.

Teaching the Lesson

- To review nouns, read aloud the relevant portions of pages 4–7 and 19–21 of the Writer's Handbook as students follow along.
- Write the following on chart paper: *Andrew plays guitar.* Have students circle the nouns. (*Andrew* and *guitar*) Ask students to determine which noun is proper and which is common. (*Andrew*, proper; *guitar*, common) Remind students that proper nouns begin with a capital letter.
- Write the following on chart paper: *Gerald's lunch included a burrito.* Have students circle the nouns. (*Gerald's, lunch, burrito*) Ask students what is special about the noun *Gerald's*. (It's possessive.) Remind students that a singular possessive noun usually ends with an apostrophe and an -s.
- Write the following on chart paper: *My sister collects stickers, and my grandpa collects old-fashioned watches.* Have a volunteer underline the singular nouns (*sister, grandpa*) and circle the plural nouns. (*stickers, watches*) Remind students that they can make most nouns plural by adding -s or -es to them.
- Write the following sentence on chart paper: *Georgia practiced cartwheels.* Have students circle the subject noun and underline the object noun. (*Georgia*, subject; *cartwheels*, object)
- Review how nouns are used. *A noun is a person, place, thing, or idea. There are many different kinds of nouns, such as common and proper, singular and plural, subject and object, and possessive.*

Extending the Lesson

Copy the paragraph in the margin onto chart paper. Have students underline all the nouns and identify each kind as proper, common, plural, singular, possessive, object, or subject. Some nouns fit in more than one category.

On Your Own

Have each student choose a page from a book in the classroom. Tell students to make a list of all the nouns they find on that page. Have them first label each noun they list as either singular or plural, then as either proper or common. Have them label the nouns as subject or object nouns. Finally, have them label any possessive nouns.

You Will Need

- Writer's Handbook, pages 4–7 and 19–21
- chart paper and marker
- paper and pencil for each student
- books for noun examples

The blue-ringed <u>octopus</u> is much more dangerous than a <u>shark</u>. This <u>octopus</u> is only the <u>size</u> of a golf <u>ball</u> but has a poisonous <u>venom</u> that can kill an <u>adult</u>. This deadly <u>creature</u> lives in the tide <u>pools</u> along <u>Australia's</u> <u>Great Barrier Reef</u>.

 **Assess Progress**

Note whether students are able to identify and differentiate between different types of nouns. Provide additional practice if necessary.

Theme 6   Review Nouns **11**

Theme 6

Action and Linking Verbs

Lesson Background

Action verbs show what the subject in a sentence does. Linking verbs do not show action, but they connect the subject to a noun or adjective in the predicate.

Teaching the Lesson

- To review action and linking verbs, read aloud the relevant portions of pages 23–24 of the Writer's Handbook as students follow along.
- Write the following sentences on chart paper: *Maria blocks the shot. She is the goalie.* Underline the verbs *blocks* and *is*. Explain that *blocks* is an action verb because it tells what Maria is doing. Then explain that the verb *is* in the second sentence is a linking verb because it does not show an action, but it does connect *she* to *goalie*, a word that describes the subject.
- As you read each of the following sentences aloud, ask students which type of verb you are using: *The tiger is an endangered species.* (*is*, linking) *Pedro built a model plane last week.* (*built*, action) *Mom made tacos for my birthday.* (*made*, action) *Henri seems upset about what happened.* (*seems*, linking)
- Explain action and linking verbs to students. *Action verbs tell what the subject of a sentence is doing. Linking verbs link the subject to a noun or an adjective in the predicate.*

Extending the Lesson

Organize students into pairs and have them work together to write two sentences that use linking verbs and two sentences that use action verbs. Share the sentences as a class.

On Your Own

Write the sentences in the margin on chart paper. Have students copy the sentences and fill in the blanks with their own words. Tell them to label each verb they choose as either *Action* or *Linking*.

You Will Need

- Writer's Handbook, pages 23–24
- chart paper and marker
- paper and pencil for each student

---

1. I ____ thrilled about my cousin's visit. [linking]
2. My friend Vera and I ____ all the way to the gym. [action]
3. Oliver ____ into the pool six times. [action]
4. Hyun ____ angry when her backpack disappeared. [linking]
5. My mom's garden ____ pretty when the flowers are in bloom. [linking]
6. Tanya ____ toward the school bus. [action]

 **Assess Progress**

Note whether students are able to differentiate between action and linking verbs. Provide additional practice if necessary.

12 Theme 6   Action and Linking Verbs

Theme 7
Main and Helping Verbs

Lesson Background
The main verb describes the action that the subject is doing in a sentence. Helping verbs can indicate the time an action occurs.

Teaching the Lesson
- To review main and helping verbs, read aloud the relevant portions of pages 23–24 of the Writer's Handbook as students follow along.
- Write the following sentence on chart paper: *American astronauts have landed on the moon six times.* Ask students to identify the main verb in the sentence. Circle *landed*. Explain that main verbs show the action the subject is doing. Say *Some sentences have helping verbs, which come before the main verb. These usually help show when the action happened.* Ask students to identify the helping verb in the sentence. Underline *have*.
- Write the following sentences on chart paper: *NASA scientists are studying the climate of Mars. We will discover more information about outer space in the future.* Have volunteers circle the main verbs and underline the helping verbs. (*studying, discover; are, will*)
- Tell students how to recognize and use main and helping verbs. *A main verb describes the action a subject is performing in a sentence. A helping verb can show the time an action occurs. Helping verbs usually come before the main verb in a sentence.*

Extending the Lesson
Tape the sentence strips to the board. Tape the index cards in random order next to the sentence strips. Work with students to place the index cards in the appropriate blanks. Have students identify the main verbs.

On Your Own
Write the sentences in the margin on chart paper. Have students copy the sentences and complete them using appropriate helping verbs. Have students circle the main verbs.

You Will Need
- Writer's Handbook, pages 23–24
- chart paper and marker
- sentence strips with the following sentences written on them:
  If a female sea turtle hatched on a certain beach, she ____ return there to lay her eggs. Humans ____ destroyed turtle nesting sites in many places. Many people ____ working to protect nesting sites all over the world.
- index cards with the following helping verbs written on them: *will, have, are*
- tape
- paper and pencil for each student

---

1. The cat ____ slept on the chair many times. [has]
2. Dad ____ work on his car this weekend. [will]
3. The fourth graders ____ finishing an art project right now. [are]
4. Ms. Tyler ____ not speak French, but she ____ speak Spanish. [does/does]
5. Students at Linda's school ____ planted a vegetable garden every year. [have]

 Assess Progress

Note whether students can identify main and helping verbs and use them correctly. Provide additional practice if necessary.

Theme 7

Past, Present, and Future Verb Tenses

Lesson Background

The past tense of a verb shows action that has already happened. The present tense of a verb shows action that is happening now. The past and present tenses can be formed by modifying the verb or adding a helping verb. The future tense shows action that has not yet happened. It is formed by adding one or more helping verbs.

Teaching the Lesson

- To review past, present, and future verb tenses, read aloud the relevant portion of page 26 of the Writer's Handbook as students follow along. You may wish to review helping verbs on page 24 as well.
- Remind students that adding a helping verb can change the time, or tense, of the action in a sentence. Say *There are three main tenses—past, present, and future.*
- Say *The past tense is when an action occurred in the past. The present tense is when an action is occurring now. The future tense is when an action will occur sometime in the future.*
- Write the following sentences on chart paper: *I played at the park last week. I play at the park now. I will play at the park tomorrow.* Point out the verb(s) in each sentence and ask students which tense each is in. (*past, present, future*)
- Tell students how to recognize tenses. *Past tense verbs show action that has already happened. Present tense verbs show action that is happening now. Future tense verbs show action that has not yet happened.*

Extending the Lesson

Choose three volunteers. Have each draw a large circle on chart paper. Ask each student to write one of the following above his or her circle: *Past Tense, Present Tense, Future Tense*. Then read the sentences in the margin aloud. Have the students listen for the verb. Ask students to determine which verbs belong in each circle, and then have the volunteers add them.

On Your Own

Have students write a few sentences in the past tense about listening to music. Then tell them to rewrite the sentences in the present tense and then in the future tense.

You Will Need

- Writer's Handbook, pages 24 and 26
- chart paper and marker
- paper and pencil for each student

---

1. People <u>brought</u> instruments to the United States from Africa. [past]
2. Some of these instruments <u>are</u> hand drums, udus, rainsticks, and djembe drums. [present]
3. Even the banjo originally <u>came</u> from Africa. [past]
4. For years musicians all over the United States <u>played</u> these instruments. [past]
5. Maybe you <u>will find</u> a concert close to you that includes African instruments! [future]

 Assess Progress

Note whether students can identify and form different verb tenses. Provide additional practice if necessary.

14 Theme 7   *Past, Present, and Future Verb Tenses*

Theme 8
Regular and Irregular Verbs

Lesson Background
Most regular verbs can be changed into the past tense by adding the suffix *-ed*. Irregular verbs cannot be formed by simply adding this suffix, so students must learn special forms of the verbs in order to form their past tense correctly.

Teaching the Lesson
- To introduce regular and irregular verbs, read aloud the relevant portions of pages 24–25 of the Writer's Handbook as students follow along.
- Tape the sentence strips to the board. Ask a volunteer to underline the verbs. Then ask students to change each sentence into past tense.
- Point out that *jump*, which is a regular verb, can be changed to past tense by adding the suffix *-ed*. Explain that some verbs, like *sing* and *speak*, change to a different form (*sang* and *spoke*) in the past tense.
- Draw the chart in the margin on chart paper. Ask several volunteers to complete the chart.
- Explain to students the difference between regular and irregular verbs. *You can change regular verbs to past tense by adding* -ed. *You must learn the past tense form of irregular verbs.*

Extending the Lesson
Write the following words on a separate piece of chart paper: *take, climb, shrink, answer, drink, swing*. Call on volunteers to create two sentences with each word, one in present tense and one in past tense. Have students label each verb as regular or irregular.

On Your Own
Have students draw their own verb tables like the one in the margin. Instruct students to look through books in the classroom to find examples of regular and irregular verbs. Tell them to add the words to their charts. Encourage students to see how many words they can find and add to their list.

You Will Need
- Writer's Handbook, pages 24–25
- chart paper and marker
- sentence strips with the following sentences written on them:
  I jump higher than my brothers.
  Susan sings songs around the campfire.
  Wai Ling speaks to his grandmother in Cantonese.
- tape
- books for examples of regular and irregular verbs
- paper and pencil for each student

Present Tense	Past Tense	Regular or Irregular
jump	jumped	regular
sing	sang	irregular
	sprang	
go		
run		
	taught	
remind		
	threw	

✓ Assess Progress
Note whether students can identify and form regular and irregular verbs. Provide additional practice if necessary.

Theme 8

Theme 8
Review Verbs

Lesson Background
Action verbs show the action the subject of a sentence performs. Linking verbs connect the subject to a word or words in the predicate that describe or rename the subject. Helping verbs can assist a main verb in indicating tense. Verbs can be in the past, present, or future tense. Regular verbs take the *-ed* suffix in the past tense, and irregular verbs must be learned.

Teaching the Lesson
- To review verbs, read aloud the relevant portions of pages 23–26 of the Writer's Handbook as students follow along.
- Write the following sentences on chart paper: *Mom cooks eggs for Mike every morning. Jason was a clown at the costume party.* Ask a volunteer to underline the verbs. Then ask students whether the verbs are action verbs or linking verbs. (*cooks*, action; *was*, linking)
- Write the following sentences on chart paper: *Marisa studies math. Jessie listened to jazz music last week.* Work with students to rewrite each sentence so it is in future tense.
- Write the following sentence on chart paper: *I will walk to school in the morning.* Have students underline the main verb (*walk*) and the helping verb. (*will*)
- Write the following words on chart paper: *draw, visit, cost, hide, collect, ride, shake, teach.* Ask students to give the past tense of each verb and record their answers. Remind students that with irregular verbs, they cannot simply add *-ed* to change the tense.
- Explain to students the proper way to use verbs. *An action verb shows action. A linking verb links a subject to a noun or adjective in the predicate. Helping verbs help main verbs show when an action happens. Verbs can be in the past, present, or future tense. Many verbs change from present to past by adding -ed. Others are irregular and have forms that must be learned.*

Extending the Lesson
Write the following words on a separate piece of chart paper: *was, drank, hike, will grow, is, shrink.* Call on volunteers to create a sentence with each word or set of words and write it on the chart paper. Ask volunteers to label each sentence with the correct tense.

On Your Own
Have students write a letter to a friend about a place they would like to visit. Tell them to use at least five verbs in their letter. Have them underline the verbs and label them *Action, Linking,* or *Helping.*

You Will Need
- Writer's Handbook, pages 23–26
- chart paper and marker
- paper and pencil for each student

Assess Progress
Note whether students can identify and differentiate between the various types and tenses of verbs. Provide additional practice if necessary.

16 Theme 8   Review Verbs

Theme 9

Subject and Object Pronouns

Lesson Background

A pronoun replaces a noun. A subject pronoun generally replaces a noun that is the subject of a sentence. An object pronoun replaces a noun that is the object in a sentence. An object pronoun usually follows an action verb or is the object of a prepositional phrase.

Teaching the Lesson

- To review subject and object pronouns, read aloud the relevant portion of page 22 of the Writer's Handbook as students follow along.
- On chart paper write *I tossed her a beanbag.* Demonstrate the sentence by tossing the beanbag to a female student. Underline *I* and say *I did the action. I tossed a beanbag. The word I is a subject pronoun.* Circle *her* and ask *Who received the action in the sentence?* ([girl's name] did, or *her*) *Because* [girl's name] *received the action in the sentence, the word* her *is an object pronoun.*
- Write *She tossed the beanbag to him.* Have students demonstrate the action and then identify the subject and object pronouns. (she, him) Explain that an object pronoun usually follows a verb or is in a prepositional phrase. In this case, the word *him* is in a prepositional phrase.
- Draw a T-chart. List subject pronouns on the left. (*I, he, she, it, we, you, they*) List object pronouns on the right. (*me, him, her, it, us, you, them*)
- Write the following sentences on chart paper: *I sent her a message. You told them to clean the room.* Have volunteers identify and underline the subject and object pronouns in each sentence. (*I*, subject; *her*, object; *You*, subject; *them*, object)
- Explain subject and object pronouns. *Subject pronouns generally replace nouns that are the subject of a sentence. Object pronouns replace object nouns and usually follow action verbs or are the object of a prepositional phrase.*

Extending the Lesson

Copy the sentences from the margin onto chart paper. Have students underline subject pronouns in red and object pronouns in blue. Not all sentences have both subject and object pronouns.

On Your Own

Ask students to select a piece of writing from their writing folder. Have them check whether they used subject and object pronouns correctly and revise their work if necessary. Then have students add a few sentences that include subject and object pronouns. Have them underline the subject pronouns in red and the object pronouns in blue.

You Will Need

- Writer's Handbook, page 22
- chart paper and marker
- small beanbag
- paper and pencil for each student
- colored pencils (red and blue) for each student

---

1. I let her go ahead. [subject, I; object, her]
2. He gave her a nice present. [subject, He; object, her]
3. She couldn't solve the crossword puzzle. [subject, She]
4. The spooky house was a mystery to us. [object, us]
5. They told the teacher about a spider. [subject, They]
6. I have a part in the school play. [subject, I]
7. We invited you to join the club. [subject, We; object, you]

 Assess Progress

Note whether students can identify and use subject and object pronouns. Provide additional practice if necessary.

Theme 9

Possessive Pronouns

Lesson Background

A possessive pronoun shows ownership. Some possessive pronouns come before a noun and modify it. These include *my, your, his, her, its, our,* and *their.* Other possessive pronouns stand alone. These include *mine, yours, his, hers, its, ours,* and *theirs.*

Teaching the Lesson

- To review possessive pronouns, read aloud the relevant portion of page 22 of the Writer's Handbook as students follow along.
- On chart paper write *That is her desk.* Point to a female student's desk. Underline the word *her* and explain that *her* is a possessive pronoun that comes before the noun. It describes the desk as the female student's. Write *That desk is hers.* Underline *hers.* Explain that *hers* is a possessive pronoun, but it stands alone. It doesn't come before a noun.
- On chart paper write *This is my desk. This desk is mine.* Have a volunteer underline the possessive pronouns on the chart paper. (*my, mine*)
- Have students create sentences using the following possessive pronouns: *her/hers, your/yours, their/theirs.* (For example, *This is her coat. The coat is hers. It is your paper. The paper is yours. That is their locker. The locker is theirs.*) Write their ideas on chart paper.
- Explain possessive pronouns. *Possessive pronouns show ownership of something. Some come before a noun and describe it, while others stand alone.*

Extending the Lesson

Copy the sentences from the margin onto chart paper. Have students identify the possessive pronouns in the sentences.

On Your Own

Have students write a short paragraph about a friend. Tell them to include at least three possessive pronouns in their paragraph.

You Will Need

- Writer's Handbook, page 22
- chart paper and marker
- paper and pencil for each student

---

1. The black computer is mine. [mine]
2. His computer is smaller, and hers is larger. [His, hers]
3. My computer cost the same amount as her new bike. [My, her]
4. How much did your computer cost? [your]
5. Our school computer is very fast, so it probably cost more than theirs did. [Our, theirs]

Assess Progress

Note whether students can identify and use possessive pronouns. Provide additional practice if necessary.

Theme 10

Singular and Plural Pronouns

Lesson Background

A pronoun replaces a noun in a sentence. A singular pronoun replaces a singular noun, which represents one person, place, thing, or idea. A plural pronoun replaces a plural noun, which represents more than one person, place, thing, or idea. This lesson focuses on singular and plural subject pronouns.

Teaching the Lesson

- To introduce singular and plural pronouns, read aloud the relevant portion of page 22 of the Writer's Handbook as students follow along.
- Explain that *singular* means "one" and *plural* means "more than one."
- Tape the first two sentence strips to the board. Identify the simple subject of the first sentence as *weather*. Explain that because the subject *weather* in the first sentence is singular, it is replaced with the singular pronoun *It* in the second sentence.
- Tape the third and fourth sentence strips to the board. Ask students to identify the simple subject of the first sentence and underline it. (*Sharks*) Explain that because the subject in the first sentence is plural, it is replaced with a plural pronoun in the second sentence. (*They*)
- List the singular pronouns (*I, you, he, she, it*) and plural pronouns (*we, you, they*) on chart paper. Write the following sentences on chart paper: *The girls walked downtown. Jason is ready to go.* Have a volunteer underline the simple subjects. (*girls, Jason*) Then have another volunteer replace the nouns with the correct pronouns. (*They, He*)
- Explain singular and plural pronouns. *Singular pronouns replace singular nouns, which represent one person, place, thing, or idea. Plural pronouns replace plural nouns, which represent more than one person, place, thing, or idea.*

Extending the Lesson

Write the sentences in the margin on chart paper. Read the sentences aloud. Then point to each of the underlined nouns. Ask students to raise one hand when they hear a singular noun and two hands when they hear a plural noun. Have volunteers come forward to the chart. Then have them replace each noun with the appropriate singular or plural pronoun.

On Your Own

Have students write a short paragraph about their family members. Tell them to use at least two singular pronouns and two plural pronouns. Have them underline the singular pronouns with one line and the plural pronouns with two lines.

You Will Need

- Writer's Handbook, page 22
- chart paper and marker
- sentence strips with the following sentences written on them:
  1. The weather was sunny and gorgeous.
  2. It was sunny and gorgeous.
  3. Sharks are ferocious animals.
  4. They are ferocious animals.
- tape
- paper and pencil for each student

---

1. The <u>cousins</u> wanted to go. [plural noun, They]
2. The <u>festival</u> was the biggest event ever. [singular noun, It]
3. Unfortunately, <u>Jim</u> couldn't go. [singular noun, he]
4. <u>Jen</u> needed to finish some homework. [singular noun, She]
5. "<u>Amos</u> and <u>I</u> will do the chores," Carla said. [plural noun, We]

 Assess Progress

Note whether students are able to replace nouns with the appropriate singular and plural pronouns. Provide additional practice if necessary.

Theme 10
Review Pronouns

Lesson Background
A pronoun replaces a noun. Personal pronouns include subject pronouns, object pronouns, and possessive pronouns. A subject pronoun is generally the subject of a sentence, and an object pronoun is the object of an action verb or a preposition. Possessive pronouns show ownership. Pronouns can be singular or plural.

Teaching the Lesson
- To review pronouns, read aloud the relevant portions of page 22 of the Writer's Handbook as students follow along.
- Draw a three-column chart on chart paper. Label the columns *Subject, Object,* and *Possessive.*
- Post the first two index cards on the board next to the chart paper. Explain that *she* is a singular subject pronoun because it can replace the subject of a sentence, as in *She ate lunch.* Place the index card in the *Subject* column.
- Repeat with the next index card. Explain that *his* is a possessive pronoun because it shows ownership of something, such as *Rusty is his dog.* Place the card in the *Possessive* column.
- Post the sentence strips on the board. Work with students to find the subject, object, and possessive pronouns. Have students write each of the pronouns on index cards and place them in the correct column on the chart. Point out that the pronoun *it* can be either an object or a subject pronoun.
- Explain the different kinds of pronouns to students. *Types of pronouns include subject, object, and possessive. Subject pronouns generally replace the subject of a sentence, object pronouns replace the object of a sentence, and possessive pronouns show ownership. Pronouns can also be singular or plural.*

Extending the Lesson
Copy the sentences from the margin onto chart paper. Have students copy the sentences and identify the types of pronouns in the sentences. Students should underline subject pronouns in red and object pronouns in blue. They should underline possessive pronouns in orange. Have students write *S* next to singular pronouns and *P* next to plural pronouns.

On Your Own
Have students write their own sentences about the upcoming weekend containing subject, object, and possessive pronouns. Have them switch papers with a partner and identify which types of pronouns are used.

You Will Need
- Writer's Handbook, page 22
- chart paper and marker
- index cards with the following pronouns and sentences written on them:
  she
  his
  I will look for your socks.
  He does not see their car.
  She found it outside.
  They realized that it was full.
- eight blank index cards
- tape
- paper and pencil for each student
- red, blue, and orange colored pencils for each student

---

1. You must return your overdue library book tomorrow. [subject: You; possessive: your]
2. We have already returned our books. [subject: We; possessive: our]
3. I returned it first thing this morning. [subject: I; object: it]

 Assess Progress

Note whether students can identify and use pronouns correctly. Provide additional practice if necessary.

Theme 11

Adjectives: Comparative and Superlative

Lesson Background

Adjectives can sometimes be comparative or superlative. A comparative adjective (*bigger*) compares two nouns and is formed by adding *-er* to the end of a one-syllable adjective. It can also be formed by adding *more* or *less* before longer adjectives. A superlative adjective (*biggest*) compares three or more nouns and is formed by adding *-est* to the end of the adjective. It can also be formed by adding *most* or *least* before longer adjectives. Some comparative and superlative adjectives are irregular and don't follow this pattern.

Teaching the Lesson

- To review comparative and superlative adjectives, read aloud the relevant portion of page 27 of the Writer's Handbook as students follow along.
- Hold up a book. Tell students the book cost one dollar. Say *I think that's cheap.* Write *cheap* on chart paper. Explain that *cheap* is an adjective because it describes a noun.
- Hold up another book and say *This book cost 50 cents.* Write *cheaper* on the chart paper and underline *-er.* Explain that a comparative adjective compares two objects and takes the suffix *-er* when it has one syllable.
- Then hold up the third book and say *This book cost only 10 cents!* Write *cheapest* on the board and underline *-est.* Explain that a superlative adjective compares three or more objects and takes the suffix *-est* when it has one syllable.
- Explain that when an adjective has more than one syllable, *more, less, most,* and *least* are usually used to form the comparative and superlative forms.
- Explain comparative and superlative adjectives. *A comparative adjective ends in -er and compares two nouns. A superlative adjective ends in -est and compares three or more nouns. When adjectives have more than one syllable,* more, less, most, *and* least *are used to form the comparative and superlative forms.*

Extending the Lesson

Copy the paragraphs from the margin onto chart paper. Have students identify the comparative and superlative adjectives and underline them. Then have volunteers write two sentences comparing different animals by using the adjectives *smart, mysterious,* and *interesting.*

On Your Own

Have students write a letter describing their own family to a friend. Tell students to use as many comparative and superlative adjectives as possible. Have them underline the comparative adjectives once and the superlative adjectives twice.

You Will Need

- Writer's Handbook, page 27
- chart paper and marker
- three books
- paper and pencil for each student

Many animals are interesting, but I believe cats are the <u>most</u> interesting of all. Domestic cats are some of the <u>tamest</u> in the cat family. Wildcats are usually ferocious and unpredictable.

A lynx is one of the <u>smallest</u> wildcats, but it is still <u>wilder</u> than a domestic cat. A male lion is the <u>largest</u> and <u>strongest</u> wildcat, but the leopard can run much <u>faster</u>. However, the cheetah is the <u>fastest</u> runner of all the cats.

Assess Progress

Note whether students can identify and use comparative and superlative adjectives correctly. Provide additional practice if necessary.

Theme 11

Adjectives: Common and Proper

Lesson Background

A proper noun is the name of a specific person, place, thing, or idea. When a word is formed from a proper noun and describes a noun, it is called a proper adjective. Like a proper noun, a proper adjective is capitalized. Common adjectives are adjectives that are not derived from proper nouns. Common adjectives are not capitalized.

Teaching the Lesson

- To introduce common and proper adjectives, read aloud the relevant portions of pages 4 and 26 of the Writer's Handbook as students follow along.
- Write the following sentence on chart paper: *Baseball is a popular American sport.* Underline *American*. Explain that *American* is capitalized because it comes from the proper noun *America* and is a proper adjective that describes *sport*. Tell students that the word *popular* is a common adjective. Say *The word* popular *describes* sport *in this sentence. Common adjectives are not capitalized.*
- Have students think of more examples of different types of proper nouns that could be used as adjectives and then use each one in a sentence. These could include names of people, nationalities, and languages. (e.g., *Shakespearean, Mexican, French*)
- Explain common and proper adjectives. *Proper adjectives are formed from proper nouns and describe nouns. They are capitalized. Common adjectives are not formed from proper nouns and are not capitalized.*

Extending the Lesson

Copy the sentences from the margin onto chart paper. Have volunteers underline the adjectives and label them as proper or common.

On Your Own

Have each student write four sentences, two with proper adjectives and two with common adjectives. Have them trade papers with a partner and label each adjective as common or proper.

You Will Need
- Writer's Handbook, pages 4 and 26
- chart paper and marker
- paper and pencil for each student

---

1. We learned about poetry in English class. [English, proper adjective]

2. "Hola" is a common Spanish word. [common, common adjective; Spanish, proper adjective]

3. Antigua is a beautiful island. [beautiful, common adjective]

4. We read Greek tragedies in history class. [Greek, proper adjective; history, common adjective]

5. I can't wait to eat Thanksgiving turkey. [Thanksgiving, proper adjective]

Assess Progress

Note whether students can identify proper and common adjectives. Provide additional practice if necessary.

Theme 12

Articles

Lesson Background
The words *a*, *an*, and *the* are articles. Articles are adjectives because they modify nouns. There are two types of articles: definite and indefinite. Indefinite articles (*a* and *an*) show that the noun modified is indefinite. These two articles can refer to any member of a group. The word *the* is a definite article. It is used when a noun is specific. *The* refers to a particular member of a group.

Teaching the Lesson
- To review articles, read aloud the tip on page 26 of the Writer's Handbook as students follow along.
- Write the following sentence on chart paper: *The boy rides a bike.* Underline *The* and *a*. Explain that the words *The* and *a* are articles. Articles can be definite or indefinite. Say *The word* the *is a definite article. In this sentence, there is a specific boy. A definite article refers to a particular member of a group. An indefinite article can refer to any member of a group.* A *and* an *are indefinite articles. There is a bike in this sentence, but we don't know which bike the boy rides.*
- Write the following sentence on chart paper: *A student read the story.* Ask students to identify each article and determine whether it is definite or indefinite. (*A* is indefinite; *the* is definite.)
- Tell students that when you use an indefinite article before a noun that begins with a vowel sound, you use the word *an*. You use the word *a* before a noun that begins with a consonant sound.
- Explain articles to students. *Articles include the words* a, an, *and* the. *Articles can be definite* (the) *or indefinite* (a *and* an).

Extending the Lesson
Copy the sentences in the margin onto chart paper. Have two or three volunteers underline the articles. Then have students label each article as definite or indefinite.

On Your Own
Have students look through books or magazines and copy one sentence for each of the following articles: *a, an,* and *the.* Students can then trade with a partner and label the articles as definite or indefinite.

You Will Need
- Writer's Handbook, page 26
- chart paper and marker
- paper and pencil for each student
- books or magazines with examples of articles

1. I am selling tickets to the school play. [the, definite]
2. It is a musical, and it has an excellent plot. [a, an, indefinite]
3. You might want to get a ticket soon. [a, indefinite]
4. The seats are filling up fast! [The, definite]
5. I have only a front-row seat left to sell. [a, indefinite]

Assess Progress
Note whether students can identify and use articles correctly. Provide additional practice if necessary.

Theme 12
Review Adjectives

Lesson Background
An adjective describes a noun or pronoun. Adjectives can be comparative or superlative. Comparative adjectives compare a noun to another noun. Superlative adjectives compare three or more nouns. Articles such as *a, an,* and *the* are also adjectives because they modify nouns or pronouns. Adjectives can also be common or proper.

Teaching the Lesson
- To review adjectives, read aloud the relevant portions of pages 4 and 26–27 of the Writer's Handbook as students follow along.
- Tape the first sentence strip to the board. Explain that *The, wonderful, English, the, youngest,* and *a* are all adjectives. *Wonderful* is a common adjective because it describes *book*. *The* and *a* are articles, and *youngest* is a superlative adjective because it compares more than two girls. *English* is a proper adjective because it is formed from a proper noun.
- Tape the second sentence strip to the board. Have students identify the articles, the comparative and superlative adjectives, and the proper adjective.
- Have students generate sentences about favorite movies and books. Write these on chart paper. Ask them to use the different types of adjectives in their sentences.
- Explain the different types of adjectives. *Adjectives modify nouns or pronouns. Adjectives can be comparative or superlative. Articles are also adjectives. Adjectives can be common or proper.*

Extending the Lesson
Copy the paragraph from the margin onto chart paper. Have students underline all the adjectives in the paragraph, including the articles.

On Your Own
Have students write a few sentences about a sport they enjoy. Then have them trade papers with a partner and underline the adjectives.

You Will Need
- Writer's Handbook, pages 4 and 26–27
- sentence strips with the following sentences written on them:
  1. *The wonderful English book is about the youngest girl to travel in a spaceship.*
  2. *The student thinks math is more interesting than science, but American history is the most interesting subject.*
- tape
- chart paper and marker
- paper and pencil for each student

Thinking about <u>a</u> career is <u>an important</u> step. <u>The best</u> way to begin is to consider what you do well. <u>Most</u> people find <u>some</u> subjects in school <u>more interesting</u> than others. Knowing what you are interested in may help you choose <u>a perfect</u> career. That is <u>the most exciting</u> part of all!

Assess Progress
Note whether students can identify and use adjectives correctly. Provide additional practice if necessary.

Theme 13
Adverbs

Lesson Background
Adverbs describe verbs, adjectives, or other adverbs. Most adverbs tell how, where, or when an action occurs. Adverbs often end in -ly.

Teaching the Lesson
- To review adverbs, read aloud the relevant portion of page 27 of the Writer's Handbook as students follow along.
- Tape the first sentence strip to the board and read it aloud. Ask *How did Maria close the door?* (quietly) Explain that *quietly* is an adverb because it tells how the action happened. Explain that many common adverbs end in -ly.
- Tape the second sentence strip to the board and read it aloud. Ask *Where did the snow fall?* (everywhere) Say *The word* everywhere *is an adverb because it tells where the action happened.*
- Tape the last sentence strip to the board and read it aloud. Ask *When did I do my homework?* (yesterday) Say *The word* yesterday *is an adverb because it tells when the action happened.*
- Draw the chart from the margin on chart paper. Have volunteers come up to the chart and write the adverbs from the sentence strips in the correct columns.
- Explain adverbs to students. *Adverbs tell how, where, or when something happens. Adverbs describe verbs, adjectives, or other adverbs.*

Extending the Lesson
As a class, brainstorm different adverbs that answer how, where, and when. Write the adverbs in the appropriate columns of the chart used in "Teaching the Lesson." If students have trouble, begin with a sentence stem such as *She rode the bike _____* . Have students tell when, where, and how she rode the bike. List the adverbs in the chart.

On Your Own
Have students write a paragraph describing their favorite weekend activity. Encourage students to include at least five adverbs in their paragraph. Have them trade papers with a partner and underline the adverbs.

You Will Need
- Writer's Handbook, page 27
- sentence strips with the following sentences written on them:
  Maria closed the door quietly.
  The snow fell everywhere.
  I did my homework yesterday.
- tape
- chart paper and marker
- paper and pencil for each student

How	Where	When

Assess Progress
Note whether students are able to identify and use adverbs. Provide additional practice if necessary.

Theme 13

Adverbs: Regular and Special Comparison Forms

Lesson Background

Adverbs describe verbs, adjectives, or other adverbs. (*fast*) A comparative adverb makes a comparison by showing more or less. It either ends in *-er* (*faster*) or is preceded by *more* or *less*. (*more skillfully*) A superlative adverb makes a comparison by showing most or least. It either ends in *-est* (*fastest*) or is preceded by *most* or *least*. (*most skillfully*)

Teaching the Lesson

- To review regular and special comparison forms of adverbs, read aloud the relevant portions of pages 27–28 of the Writer's Handbook as students follow along.
- Explain to students that some adverbs show comparison. These adverbs show the differences between qualities.
- Write the following on chart paper: *Dominik arrived earlier than Jacob did*. Explain that *earlier* is a comparative adverb because it compares when Dominik arrived to when Jacob arrived. Tell students that to form comparative adverbs, you add *-er* to adverbs with one syllable and use *more* or *less* before most adverbs with two or more syllables.
- Write the following on chart paper: *Tracy runs fastest of all the students in her class*. Explain that *fastest* is a superlative adverb because it compares how Tracy runs to all the other students in her class. To form superlative adverbs, add *-est* to adverbs with one syllable and use *most* or *least* before most longer adverbs.
- Write the following on chart paper: *I like Brussels sprouts best*. Explain that *best* is an adverb because it describes the verb *like*. Tell students that some adverbs do not follow the rules.
- Explain the different adverb forms. *Adverbs tell how, where, or when an action happens. Comparative adverbs make a comparison showing more or less. Superlative adverbs make comparisons showing most or least.*

Extending the Lesson

Write the sentences in the margin on chart paper. Have students copy the sentences onto their own paper and change each adjective into the correct form of adverb to complete the sentences.

On Your Own

Have students write sentences describing how they exercise. Encourage students to use at least two comparative adverbs and two superlative adverbs. Have partners trade papers and underline the adverbs.

You Will Need

- Writer's Handbook, pages 27–28
- chart paper and marker
- paper and pencil for each student

---

1. The cat sleeps _____ on the couch. (quiet) [quietly]
2. The dog _____ chases squirrels. (quick) [quickly]
3. I arrived _____ than anyone else at the party. (early) [earlier]
4. Marla played _____ at her recital. (beautiful) [beautifully]
5. I study _____ than my brother. (hard) [harder]
6. Connor pitches _____ of all the players on the team. (fast) [fastest]
7. Alison is the _____ of all the workers. (success) [most successful]

 Assess Progress

Note whether students are able to identify and use different forms of adverbs correctly. Provide additional practice if necessary.

---

26 Theme 13 — Adverbs: Regular and Special Comparison Forms

Theme 14
Contractions

Lesson Background

A contraction is the shortened form of two words. The two words are combined, and one or more letters are removed. An apostrophe is used in place of the removed letter or letters. Formal writing requires that contractions be spelled out. Contractions are used to make informal writing resemble speech.

Teaching the Lesson

- To review contractions, read aloud the relevant portion of page 18 of the Writer's Handbook as students follow along.
- Write the following sentence on chart paper: *Miguel didn't go to the soccer game.* Ask students to identify the contraction. Explain that *didn't* means the same as *did not*. It is the shortened form of the two words. Ask students to identify which letter has been removed. (*o*) Remind students that *didn't* is the informal version of *did not*.
- Read aloud the following sentence: *We don't have any oranges.* Explain that *don't* is a contraction of the words *do not*. Point out that *do* and *not* have different sounds than *don't*. The *o* sound in *do* and *don't* is different. Remind students that *don't* is the informal version of *do not*.
- Write the following contractions on chart paper: *I've, shouldn't, it's, they'll.* Have students identify the words that form each contraction.
- Tell students that there are irregular contractions that don't look like the original two words. Write the following sentence on chart paper: *We won't be able to go.* Have a volunteer underline the contraction. (*won't*) Ask *What two words make up the contraction* won't? (*will not*) Say *The contraction looks different from the two words that we combined to make it.*
- Explain how to form contractions. *Contractions are shortened versions of two words that are put together. An apostrophe is used in place of the removed letter or letters.*

Extending the Lesson

Copy the paragraphs from the margin onto chart paper. Have students underline words in the story that can form contractions. Tell students to replace the underlined word or words with a contraction. Ask volunteers to read the story aloud after revising it.

On Your Own

Have students select a recent piece of writing from their writing folder. Ask them to revise the writing by removing the contractions and replacing them with the original word or words.

You Will Need

- Writer's Handbook, page 18
- chart paper and marker
- paper and pencil for each student

Louisa <u>could</u> <u>not</u> wait for the lunar eclipse. "<u>I am</u> so excited! I <u>cannot</u> sleep because I <u>do</u> <u>not</u> want to miss the eclipse!"

It grew late, and Louisa rubbed her eyes. "<u>I am</u> falling asleep now," she said. Soon she <u>could</u> <u>not</u> stay awake.

Her mother said, "The eclipse <u>will</u> <u>not</u> be for another hour. Take a nap and <u>I will</u> wake you when <u>it is</u> time."

 Assess Progress

Note whether students are able to identify and use contractions. Provide additional practice if necessary.

Theme 14   *Contractions* **27**

Theme 14

Prepositions and Prepositional Phrases

Lesson Background
Prepositions show the relation of a noun or a pronoun to another word in a sentence. A prepositional phrase includes the preposition, an object of the preposition, and all descriptive words in between.

Teaching the Lesson
- To review prepositions and prepositional phrases, read aloud the relevant portion of page 28 of the Writer's Handbook as students follow along.
- Tape the chart paper with the drawing of a tree on it to the board. Explain that the tree is the object. Tape a bird above the tree. Write the prepositional phrase *above the tree* next to the bird on the paper. Explain that the word *above* is a preposition because it tells where the bird is in relation to the tree.
- Explain that *above the tree* is a prepositional phrase. It contains the preposition *above* and the object *tree*. *Tree* is the object of the preposition because it is the noun that follows the preposition and shows which object the bird is above.
- Explain that some prepositions may not show direction. These include *for, by, of,* and *with*. Have students think of sentences that use each of these prepositions. Write each sentence on chart paper and enclose the prepositional phrase in parentheses.
- Explain to students that prepositions show the relation of one object to another. *A preposition often shows the relation of a noun or a pronoun to another word in a sentence. A prepositional phrase includes the preposition, the object of the preposition, and all words in between.*

Extending the Lesson
As a class, continue taping animals on various places around the tree. Write prepositional phrases describing the location of each of the animals. (*e.g., below the tree, in the tree*)

On Your Own
Copy the sentences in the margin onto chart paper. Have students copy the sentences onto their own paper. Then have them underline the prepositions. Students should enclose the complete prepositional phrases in parentheses. If students have trouble, include the number of prepositional phrases at the end of the sentence.

You Will Need
- Writer's Handbook, page 28
- chart paper and marker
- drawing of a tree without leaves on chart paper
- paper cut into the following shapes: bird, squirrel, worm, dog
- tape
- paper and pencil for each student

---

1. Cindy put her homework (<u>in</u> her backpack). (1)
2. I gave a card (<u>to</u> Safiya) (<u>for</u> her birthday). (2)
3. Eddy saw a chipmunk run (<u>up</u> a water pipe) and (<u>into</u> the window) (<u>of</u> a house)! (3)
4. The llama climbed (<u>up</u> the mountain) (<u>with</u> packs) (<u>on</u> its back). (3)

 Assess Progress

Note whether students are able to identify prepositions and prepositional phrases. Provide additional practice if necessary.

Theme 15

Conjunctions: Coordinate and Subordinate

Lesson Background

A conjunction joins two or more words or groups of words. A coordinate conjunction, such as *and*, connects words or grammatically equal clauses or phrases. A subordinate conjunction, such as *before*, joins two clauses to form a complex sentence.

Teaching the Lesson

- To review coordinate and subordinate conjunctions, read aloud the relevant portion of page 29 of the Writer's Handbook as students follow along.
- Remind students that conjunctions join words or groups of words.
- List the coordinate conjunctions on chart paper: *for, and, or, nor, but, yet, so.* Then write the following sentence on chart paper and work with students to complete it: *Lisa wanted to visit the beach _____ the mountains.* (and, or) Explain that the words *and* and *or* connect equal parts of a sentence.
- Tape the first two sentence strips to chart paper. Explain that these two sentences can be joined by the coordinate conjunction *so*. (*My room is messy, so I must clean it.*)
- List some subordinate conjunctions on chart paper: *after, because, before, if, since,* etc. Then work with students to complete this sentence: *I had to study hard _____ I took my test.* [before] Explain that a subordinate conjunction shows that one part of a sentence depends on the other part.
- Tape the last two sentence strips to the chart paper. Explain that these two sentences can be joined with the subordinate conjunction *unless*. (*I cannot go to the park unless I wash the dishes.*)
- Explain the different types of conjunctions to students. *A coordinate conjunction connects words or grammatically equal clauses or phrases. A subordinate conjunction joins two clauses to show that one part of the sentence depends on the other part.*

Extending the Lesson

Copy the sentences from the margin onto chart paper. Tell students to underline each conjunction. Have students identify whether the conjunction is coordinate or subordinate.

On Your Own

Tape the chart paper with the different conjunctions from "Teaching the Lesson" to the board. Have students write a short paragraph about visiting their favorite place. Tell students to use coordinate and subordinate conjunctions to link their ideas.

You Will Need
- Writer's Handbook, page 29
- chart paper and marker
- sentence strips with the following written on them:
  My room is messy.
  I must clean it.
  I cannot go to the park.
  I wash the dishes.
- tape
- paper and pencil for each student

---

1. I cannot see well until I put on my glasses. [subordinate]

2. The dog jumps up when the mail carrier passes our gate. [subordinate]

3. My grandfather likes to take walks, yet he gets tired easily. [coordinate]

4. I do not dance, but I do sing. [coordinate]

5. Orson got a role in a high school play, though he is only in fifth grade. [subordinate]

 Assess Progress

Note whether students are able to use coordinate and subordinate conjunctions correctly. Provide additional practice if necessary.

Theme 15

Independent and Dependent Clauses

Lesson Background

A clause is a group of words that includes a subject and a predicate. An independent clause contains a subject and a predicate and expresses a complete thought. An independent clause can stand alone as a simple sentence. A dependent clause does not express a complete thought and cannot stand alone as a sentence.

Teaching the Lesson

- To introduce independent and dependent clauses, read aloud the relevant portion of page 36 of the Writer's Handbook as students follow along.
- Write the following on chart paper: *When Josey wore a jacket to the football game.* Ask students *Is this a complete sentence?* (no) Explain that this clause is dependent because it does not express a complete thought.
- Work with students to rewrite the sentence to make it complete. (*When Josey wore a jacket to the football game, she stayed warm.*) Remind students that the sentence now expresses a complete thought. It contains a dependent clause (*When Josey wore a jacket to the football game*) and an independent clause. (*she stayed warm*)
- Tape the sentence strips to the board. Ask students to identify whether the clauses are independent or dependent.
- Explain independent and dependent clauses to students. *An independent clause is a complete sentence because it expresses a complete thought. A dependent clause does not express a complete thought and cannot stand alone as a sentence.*

Extending the Lesson

Write the clauses from the margin on chart paper. Have volunteers label each clause as dependent or independent. As a class, rewrite each dependent clause so that it is part of a sentence that expresses a complete thought.

On Your Own

Have students select a recent piece of writing from their writing folder that needs editing. Have students trade with a partner. Ask students to edit any dependent clauses so that they are independent clauses.

You Will Need

- Writer's Handbook, page 36
- chart paper and marker
- sentence strips with the following written on them:
  I made my dad some spaghetti.
  As you ran.
  We softly hummed a song.
  I ate a sandwich.
  Since I was tired.
- tape
- paper and pencil for each student

---

1. My mom threw a ball to my sister. [independent]
2. Although it was equal. [dependent]
3. When they go fishing. [dependent]
4. I ran toward you. [independent]
5. I was sad. [independent]

 Assess Progress

Note whether students are able to identify dependent and independent clauses. Provide additional practice if necessary.

Theme 16

Homophones

Lesson Background

Homophones are words with the same pronunciation but with different meanings and different spellings. The words *threw* and *through* are examples of homophones.

Teaching the Lesson

- To review homophones, read aloud the relevant portion of page 31 and a few examples of homophones from pages 50–54 of the Writer's Handbook as students follow along.
- Tape the sentence strips to the board and read them aloud. Underline *threw* and *through*. Explain to students that *threw* and *through* are homophones. The two words sound the same but have different spellings and meanings.
- List the following sets of homophones on chart paper: *in* and *inn*, *heal* and *heel*, *hole* and *whole*, *flour* and *flower*. Review the meaning of each word. Have students use each word in a sentence.
- Have students fold a sheet of paper in half. Then have them choose one of the pairs of homophones to illustrate. They should draw one homophone on the left and the other homophone on the right. Have students exchange papers and challenge partners to guess the homophones.
- Explain homophones to students. *Homophones are words with the same pronunciation but with different meanings and different spellings.*

Extending the Lesson

As a class, brainstorm four more sets of homophones. Write them on chart paper. Discuss the meanings of the homophones. Have students write sentences for each set of homophones. Use the following as an example: <u>Our</u> dinner cooked for an <u>hour</u>. Have students write their sentences on chart paper.

On Your Own

Have students look through books or magazines you have in the classroom to find and list four more sets of homophones on index cards. Have students draw or describe a picture that uses both homophones, such as a *pair* of *pears*.

You Will Need

- Writer's Handbook, pages 31 and 50–54
- sentence strips with the following sentences written on them:
  José threw the ball to the pitcher.
  Sheila ran through the field of flowers.
- tape
- chart paper and marker
- paper, pencil, and drawing materials for each student
- books or magazines with homophone examples
- four index cards for each student

Assess Progress

Note whether students can identify and use homophones correctly. Provide additional practice if necessary.

Theme 16

Commonly Misused Words

Lesson Background

Some words sound the same or similar and are often confused with one another. Although the words sound similar, they are spelled differently and have different meanings. An example of a set of commonly misused words is *than* and *then*.

Teaching the Lesson

- To introduce commonly misused words, read aloud a few examples from pages 50–54 of the Writer's Handbook as students follow along.
- Write the following words on chart paper: *lose/loose, chose/choose, to/too/two, there/their/they're*. Explain to students that these words are often confused with one another. Discuss the meaning of each word as a class and have volunteers use each word in a sentence. Write the definitions and example sentences on chart paper.
- Write *accept* and *except* on chart paper. Explain the definitions of these two words and have students use each word correctly in a sentence.
- Discuss the importance of understanding the different meanings and uses of these words. Say *Looking at the other words in a sentence can help you understand which word to use.*
- Explain to students that some words that sound similar are commonly misused. *Words that sound similar can often be confusing. It is important to be familiar with the different meanings and spellings of these words.*

Extending the Lesson

Copy the sentences in the margin onto chart paper. Then have students copy these onto their own paper. Have students choose the correct word for each sentence.

On Your Own

Encourage students to look at the list of commonly misused words on pages 50–54 of the Writer's Handbook to find a set that is difficult for them. Then have students make a saying or an illustration that will help them remember the difference between the two words. Tape students' papers to the wall to help them throughout the year.

You Will Need

- Writer's Handbook, pages 50–54
- chart paper and marker
- paper, pencil, and drawing materials for each student
- tape

---

1. Our (principle/principal) taught fifth grade (four/for) ten years. [principal, for]
2. I didn't think the test would (affect/effect) my grade. [affect]
3. The dog hurt (its/it's) leg. [its]
4. (Then/Than) I told her that I like chocolate better (then/than) vanilla. [Then, than]
5. What is (your/you're) favorite kind of (desert/dessert)? [your, dessert]
6. (They're/There/Their) books are over (they're/there/their). [Their, there]

 Assess Progress

Note whether students are able to correctly use commonly misused words. Provide additional practice if necessary.

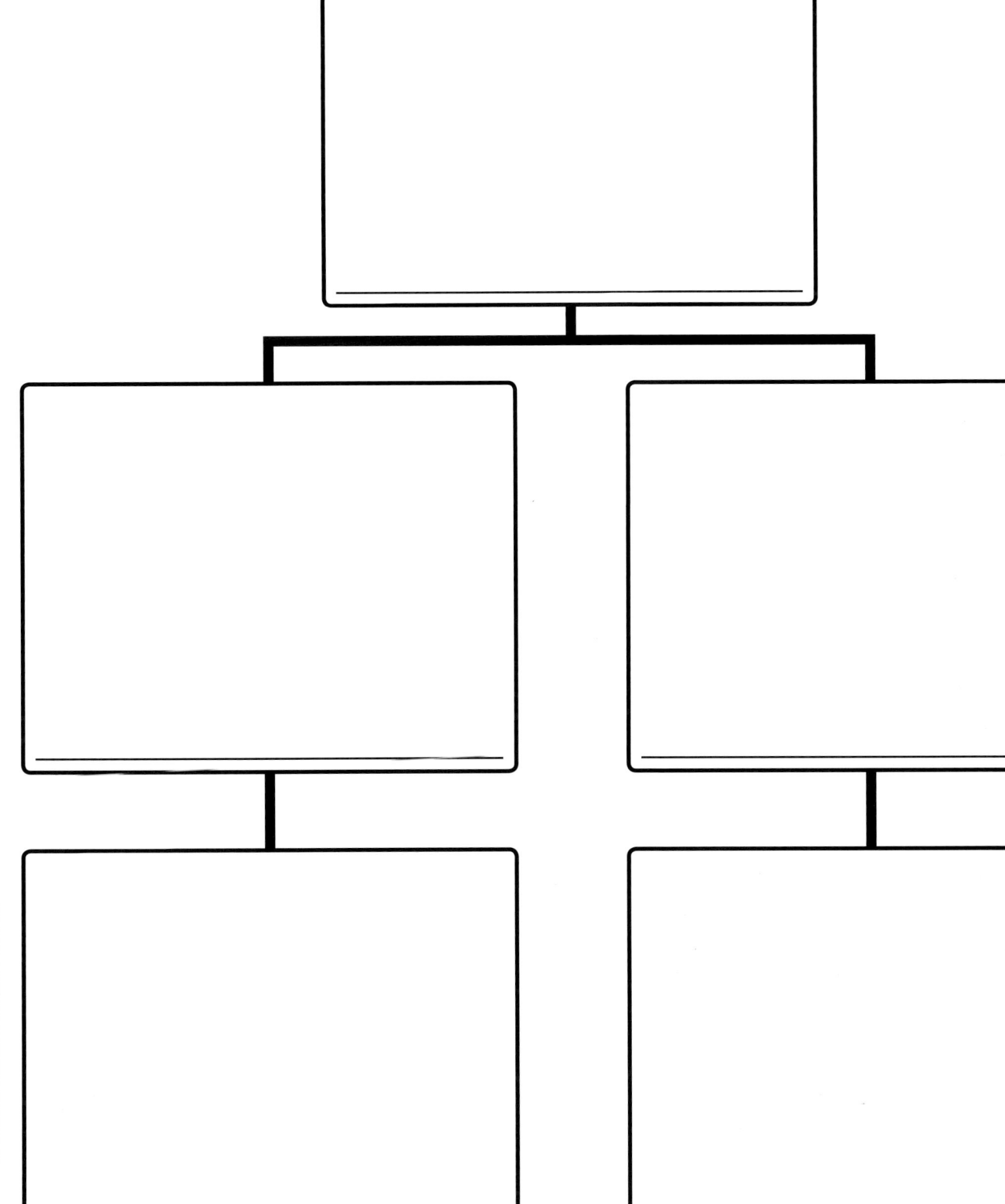

Name _____   Date _____

Main Idea and Details Organizer

Theme 1   Main Idea and Details Organizer **33**

Name _____   Date _____

Story Organizer

Title

Setting

Characters

Problem

Events
1.
2.
3.

Solution

Ending

Name_____ Date_____

Sequence Organizer

First
_____
_____
_____

Second
_____
_____
_____

Next
_____
_____
_____

Then
_____
_____
_____

Then
_____
_____
_____

Last
_____
_____
_____

Theme 3

Name_____ Date _____

Poem Organizer

Image	Descriptive Words
	_____ _____ _____ _____ _____ _____ _____
	_____ _____ _____ _____ _____ _____ _____
	_____ _____ _____ _____ _____ _____ _____

Name _____ Date _____

Biography Organizer

Person: _____

Key Life Events

Theme 5

Biography Organizer **37**

Name_____ Date_____

Problem and Solution Organizer

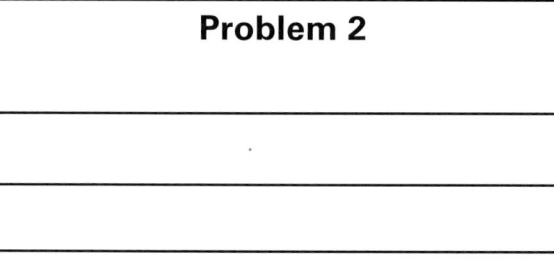

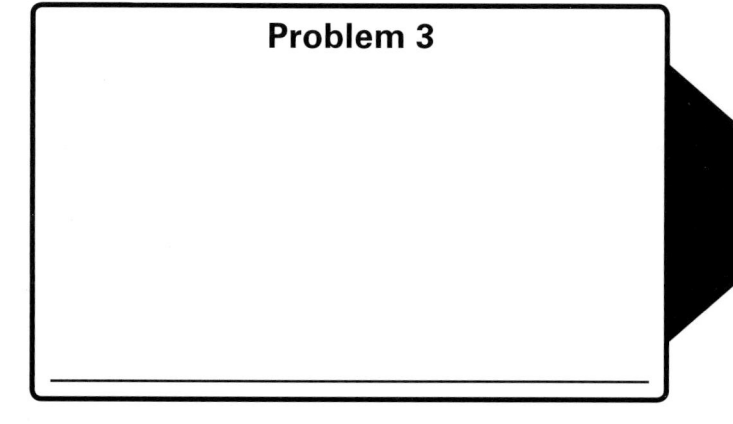

Problem 1	Solution

Problem 2	Solution

Problem 3	Solution

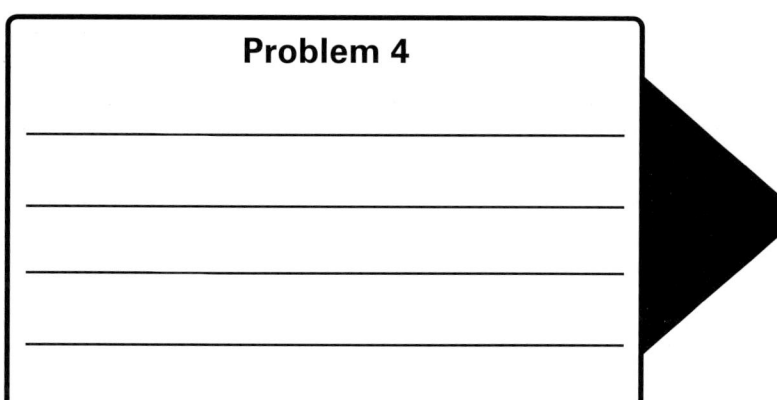

Problem 4	Solution

Name _____ Date _____

Newspaper Article Organizer

Title: _____

5 Ws

Who?	

What?	

When?	

Where?	

Why?	

Name_____ Date_____

Cause and Effect Organizer

Sunday		
	Monday	
	Tuesday	
	Wednesday	

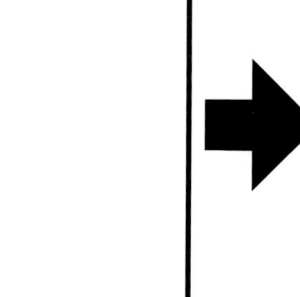
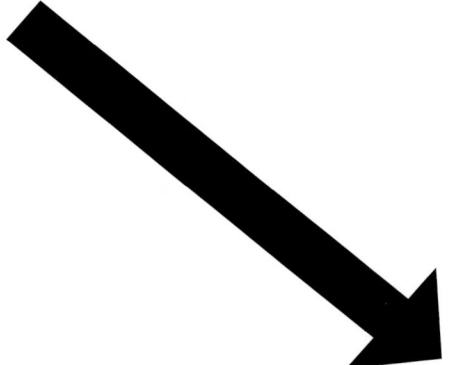

Name _____ Date _____

Report Organizer

Main Idea

_____

Supporting Detail

_____
_____
_____
_____

Supporting Detail

_____
_____
_____
_____

Supporting Detail

_____
_____
_____
_____

Conclusion

_____
_____

Theme 9   Report Organizer

Name_____ Date_____

Sequence Organizer

Step 1

Step 2

Step 3

Step 4

Step 5

Name _____   Date _____

Observation Log Organizer

Time ↓	Object	Place ↓
Description →		
Changes →		

Time ↓	Object	Place ↓
Description →		
Changes →		

Time ↓	Object	Place ↓
Description →		
Changes →		

Theme 11   Observation Log Organizer **43**

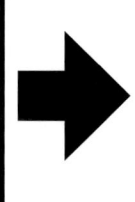

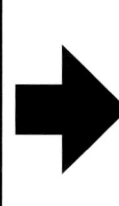

Name_____ Date_____

Sequence Organizer

Step 1	Step 2
Step 3	Step 4
Step 5	Step 6

Name _____   Date _____

Persuasive Essay Organizer

What I Think

_____
_____
_____

Reason 1

_____
_____
_____
_____

Reason 2

_____
_____
_____
_____

Reason 3

_____
_____
_____
_____

Theme 13　　　　　　　　　　　　　　　　　　Persuasive Essay Organizer

Name_____   Date_____

Compare and Contrast Organizer

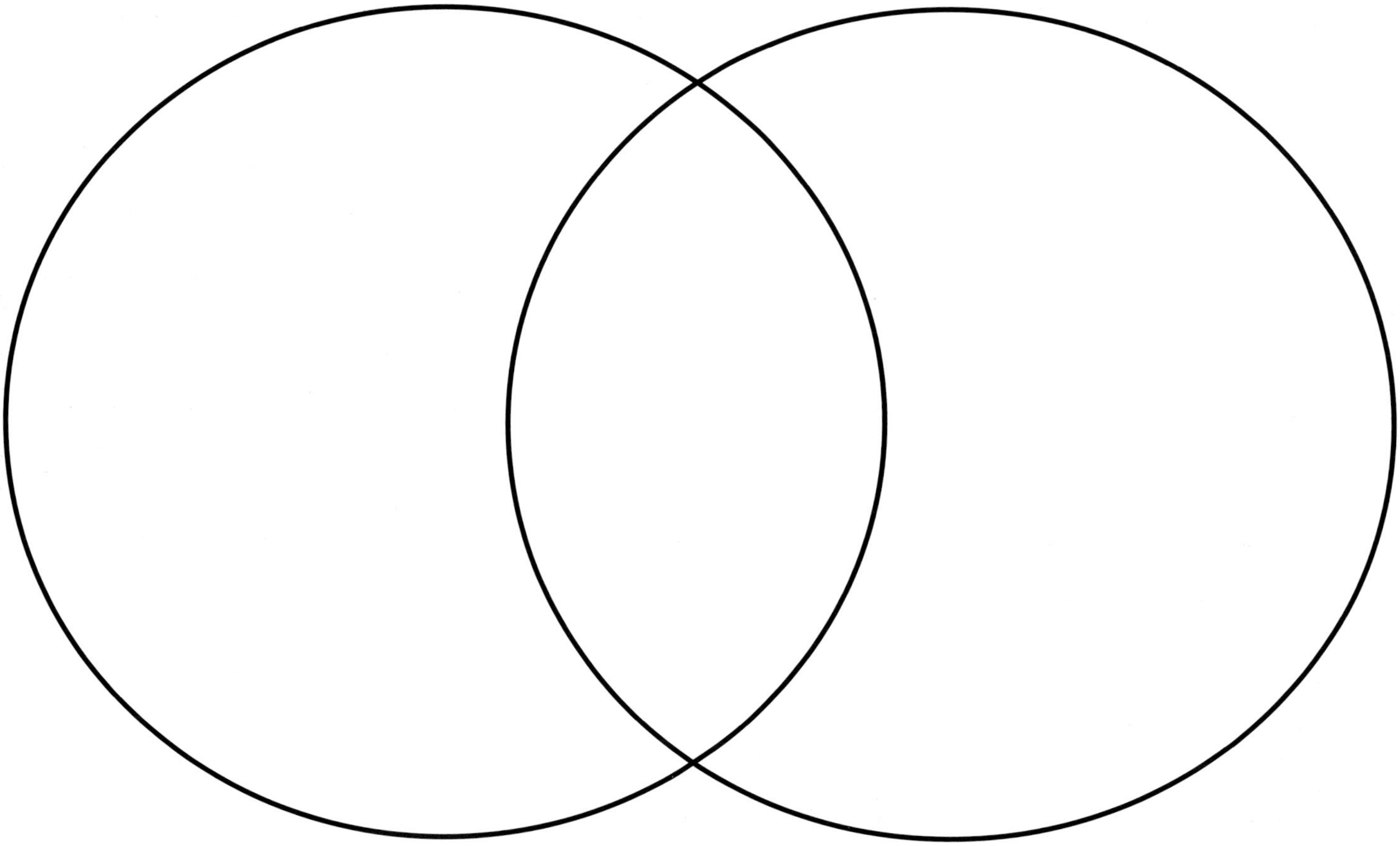

Name _____   Date _____

Letter Organizer

Date

Salutation

Body

Closing

Theme 15   Letter Organizer **47**

Name _____ Date _____

Story Organizer

Title

Setting

Characters

Problem

Events

1. _____
2. _____
3. _____

Solution

Ending

Writer's Craft — Build Suspense in Fiction

Keep Your Reader Guessing

Lesson Background
Interesting stories build suspense through a series of events that keep readers on the edge of their seat, present a warning about the future, or introduce an unexpected twist in the plot. An effective story makes readers want to continue reading. Introduce suspense in fiction by having students learn about stories with unexpected twists.

Teaching the Lesson
- Copy and distribute the Build Suspense in Fiction Master on page 50 of this guide. You may wish to make a transparency of this page for use during whole-class instruction.
- Read the selection "Rosa's Adventure" aloud as students follow along.
- After reading, discuss the selection with students. *Do you want to know what happens to Rosa?* (yes) *Are you wondering why she suddenly had to take a trip?* (yes) *Which words or phrases in the story help keep you guessing?* (*a flight to Rome, the big event, she overslept*)
- Tell students that writers help readers stay interested in a story by keeping them guessing about what will happen next. This is called suspense. Some writers add an unexpected twist at the end to make a story more interesting. As a class, brainstorm a list of unexpected twists that could happen at the end of "Rosa's Adventure." You might wish to suggest the following ideas for endings: *Rosa finds out that her flight has been cancelled. Rosa finds out that the important event was moved to London.*
- Have students write an ending for "Rosa's Adventure" that adds an unexpected twist. They may record a class suggestion or write an unexpected ending of their own.

Extending the Lesson
During small-group writing instruction, have students select a recent piece of writing from their writing folder that they think needs a more suspenseful or unexpected ending. Support students as they revise their writing. Then compare the original and revised versions as a group.

On Your Own
Have students look through other fiction texts to find unexpected endings that engage the reader. Encourage students to record some of these examples in their Writer's Notebook as a resource for ways to insert suspense in a story.

Assess Progress

Note whether students are able to craft a story with an unexpected twist at the end. Provide additional practice if necessary.

Rosa's Adventure

When Rosa heard the news last night, she immediately called her assistant Louis and told him to book a flight to Rome. She didn't want to miss the big event. There weren't any flights leaving until morning, but Louis got her on the first flight out. However, she was so tired that she overslept! She tossed random items into her suitcase, desperately trying to remember everything she would need. Her plane was scheduled to leave in one hour, so she wildly ran to her car. When she got to the airport, there was a huge line in front of her.

Write an Unexpected Ending

Write an ending for "Rosa's Adventure" that adds an unexpected twist.

_____
_____
_____
_____
_____
_____
_____

Writer's Craft — Include Figurative Language

Create a Unique Vision

Lesson Background
Many stories include figurative language to make the writing more interesting. Adding symbolism gives a piece deeper meaning and helps readers connect with what they read. This lesson focuses on the strategy of adding symbolism to a piece of fiction or poetry.

Teaching the Lesson
- Copy and distribute the Include Figurative Language Master on page 52 of this guide. You may wish to make a transparency of this page for use during whole-class instruction.
- Read the selection "Nature Song" aloud as students follow along.
- After reading, discuss the selection with students. *What genre is "Nature Song"?* (a poem) *What is the subject of the piece?* (trees and the seasons) *What words help you create a picture in your mind while reading this poem?* (encircled her tiny yard, stretching their long arms) *How is Jordan like the trees?* (She is growing up, too.)
- Tell students that using figurative language will make their writing unique and interesting. Explain that a symbol is something that stands for, or represents, something else. Ask students what they think the color red represents. (fire, heat, danger, love) Then ask what a tree might symbolize. (wisdom, strength, age) Have students identify and discuss the symbolism of the seasons in "Nature Song." As a class, brainstorm ways to add symbolism to the poem.
- Have students edit "Nature Song" by adding more symbolism. They may incorporate a class suggestion or include a symbol of their own.

Extending the Lesson
During small-group writing instruction, have students select a recent poem or story from their writing folder that they think could be improved by adding symbolism. Support students as they revise their writing. Then compare the original and revised versions as a group.

On Your Own
Have students look through books for examples of symbolism. Encourage students to record some of these examples in their Writer's Notebook as a resource for how to include symbolism in their writing.

Assess Progress

Note whether students are able to add symbolism to their writing. Provide additional practice if necessary.

Nature Song

Young Jordan watched
as the ancient trees grew
and encircled her tiny yard.
Each year they got taller,
stretching their long arms
toward the warm, bright sun.

She watched the golden leaves
gently flutter down in autumn
so that new life bloomed in the spring.
Jordan could always rely on her friends
to shade her on scorching summer days.

Use Symbolism
Write a line or stanza that uses symbolism and add it to "Nature Song."

_____
_____
_____
_____
_____

 **Build Characters**

Breathe Life into the People in Your Stories

Lesson Background
Strong characters bring life to stories. Writers build characters through dialogue between characters as well as through description, action, or the narrator's opinions. This lesson focuses on the strategy of building characters by showing the reactions of other characters.

Teaching the Lesson
- Copy and distribute the Build Characters Master on page 54 of this guide. You may wish to make a transparency of this page for use during whole-class instruction.
- Read the selection "Home Run Hitter" aloud as students follow along.
- After reading, discuss the selection with students. *Who is the main character of this passage?* (Danny) *How are the other characters connected to the main character?* (They are at his baseball game.) *How does the reader learn how other characters react?* (by reading what they say)
- Tell students that one way writers develop characters in a story is by showing how other characters react to them through dialogue or description. Ask *When you read "Home Run Hitter," do you get the sense that Danny is a good baseball player?* (No) *Why?* (Javier tells us he didn't do well in another game.) As a class, brainstorm ways to show reactions of other characters in the story. You might suggest the following: *How did Danny's opponents react to him? How did the crowd react?*
- Have students edit "Home Run Hitter" by describing Danny through the other characters' reactions. They may record a class suggestion or write about other character reactions on their own.

Extending the Lesson
During small-group writing instruction, have students select a recent piece of writing from their writing folder that they think needs more character development. Support students as they revise their writing to include more character action and the reactions of other characters. Then compare the original and revised versions as a group.

On Your Own
Have students look through other fiction and nonfiction texts to find well-developed characters. Encourage students to record some of these examples in their Writer's Notebook as a resource for how to build characters.

 **Assess Progress**

Note whether students are able to show how characters' reactions describe the main character in their own writing. Provide additional practice if necessary.

Home Run Hitter

It was the ninth inning. There were two outs, and it was Danny's turn at bat. He hesitated. His friend Javier noticed that Danny was chewing the fingernails on his left hand. Javier patted Danny on the shoulder.

"Danny," Javier said. "I know you're nervous. Forget about what happened before. You can do it!"

Danny stepped up to the plate. The coach saw Danny plant his feet firmly into the ground and brace himself for the pitch. As the ball came toward him, he swung his bat as hard as he could.

Crack! "Yes!" Danny yelled. He watched the ball fly toward the crowd.

"Go, Danny, go!" his coach yelled.

As he rounded third base, Danny heard his teammates yelling excitedly, "You got it, Danny. You hit a home run!"

Show a Reaction

Add another sentence or two to the end of the story that shows how others react to Danny in "Home Run Hitter."

_____

_____

_____

 **Start Strong**

Engage Your Reader with a Lively Beginning

Lesson Background
Drawing readers in with an interesting beginning sentence or paragraph is the best way to engage them. Ways to engage the reader from the beginning include presenting an interesting detail about the topic, asking a question, opening with a sensory image, or presenting the big picture. This lesson focuses on starting strong by presenting an interesting detail.

Teaching the Lesson
- Copy and distribute the Start Strong Master on page 56 of this guide. You may wish to make a transparency of this page for use during whole-class instruction.
- Read the selection "Curious Cats" aloud as students follow along.
- After reading, discuss the selection with students. *What was good about this piece of writing?* (It contained a lot of details.) *Did the opener of the piece make you want to read more?* (no) *What would you improve about this piece of writing?* (I would make the beginning more interesting.)
- Tell students that the beginning of a piece of writing should draw the reader in and make him or her want to keep reading. One way writers can engage readers from the beginning is to present an interesting detail about the topic. As a class, brainstorm possible details that would engage the reader in the opening of "Curious Cats." You might suggest the following: *The Egyptians first kept cats as pets 4,000 years ago. Cats have changed little since then.*
- Have students revise "Curious Cats" to include an interesting detail in the opener. They may record a class suggestion or write an opener of their own.

Extending the Lesson
During small-group writing instruction, have students select a recent piece of writing from their writing folder that they think needs a stronger beginning. Support students as they revise their writing. Then compare the original and revised versions as a group.

On Your Own
Have students look through other fiction texts to find openers that present an interesting detail that engages the reader. Encourage students to record some of these in their Writer's Notebook as examples of effective openers.

 **Assess Progress**

Note whether students are able to craft strong openers in their writing by presenting an interesting detail. Provide additional practice if necessary.

Writer's Craft · Start Strong **55**

Curious Cats

Cats come in many shapes, sizes, and colors. They also live all over the world. The cat family has an amazing range of colors and patterns. Some cats have stripes or spots, while others are one solid color. Cats have very strong senses. Even if a room is very dark, they know where they are going by using their powerful eyes and whiskers. Cats are easy to care for because they clean themselves. Unlike dogs, cats don't need to go outside for a walk. They get plenty of exercise by playing indoors. Sometimes, cats will cuddle with their owners, but other times they like to be left alone. Cats have made great pets for many centuries.

Write a Strong Beginning

Write a more interesting opener for "Curious Cats" by presenting an interesting detail.

_____
_____
_____
_____

Build Strong Paragraphs

Make Your Ideas Clear

Lesson Background
Strong paragraphs are the building blocks of a piece of writing. To build strong paragraphs, it is important to focus them, write a strong topic sentence, use supporting details, and include transitions between ideas. This lesson focuses on building strong paragraphs by using transitions between ideas.

Teaching the Lesson
- Copy and distribute the Build Strong Paragraphs Master on page 58 of this guide. You may wish to make a transparency of this page for use during whole-class instruction.
- Read the selection "Planting a Garden" aloud as students follow along.
- After reading, discuss the selection with students. *Was each step in the selection easy to follow?* (yes) *Did each of the ideas go together?* (yes) *What would you do to improve the selection so it is easier to follow?* (I would explain the order in which the steps happened by using transitions.)
- Tell students that strong paragraphs make a piece of writing successful. Explain that within each paragraph, transitions, such as *first*, *next*, and *then*, should guide the reader from one thought to the next. As a class, brainstorm ways to include additional transitions in "Planting a Garden." You might suggest students use time order words or cause and effect words as transitions.
- Have students revise "Planting a Garden" to include transitions that guide the reader. They may record a class suggestion or rewrite the paragraph with transitions of their own.

Extending the Lesson
During small-group writing instruction, have students select a recent piece of writing from their writing folder that they think needs more transitions. Support students as they revise their writing. Then compare the original and revised versions as a group.

On Your Own
Have students look through other fiction and nonfiction texts to find transitions that guide the reader through the writing. Encourage students to record some of these in their Writer's Notebook as a resource for ways to build strong paragraphs.

Assess Progress

Note whether students are able to craft a strong paragraph using transitions. Provide additional practice if necessary.

Writer's Craft

Planting a Garden

I decided to plant a garden in my backyard, but I had to prepare a space before I could do anything else. I divided my garden into sections by using long pieces of wood. I used a shovel to loosen up the dirt. I decided where to plant each kind of seed that I bought. I put the seeds in the ground and covered them with dirt. I watered the seeds and waited for them to grow.

Use Transitions

Rewrite the passage "Planting a Garden" by inserting transitions between ideas.

_____
_____
_____
_____
_____
_____
_____

Writer's Craft — Keep Language Fresh

Use Active Words and Phrases

Lesson Background
Writing is more direct and lively when writers keep their language fresh by using active voice instead of passive voice. It is also important to avoid cliches and empty adjectives. This lesson focuses on keeping language fresh by using action words and avoiding passive voice.

Teaching the Lesson
- Copy and distribute the Keep Language Fresh Master on page 60 of this guide. You may wish to make a transparency of this page for use during whole-class instruction.
- Read the selection "The Last Game" aloud as students follow along.
- After reading, discuss the selection with students. *Does the story have a lot of action in it?* (yes) *Do you think the story is interesting and lively?* (yes) *How do you think this story could be improved?* (by making the passive sentences active)
- Tell students that in the active voice the subject performs the action expressed in the verb. In the passive voice, the subject receives the action expressed in the verb. Read the following sentence from the story aloud: *The game was won!* Ask *Who won the game?* (It's not clear.) Explain that you know which team won the game, so you could change the sentence to *Kelly's team won the game!*
- As a class, brainstorm ways to make "The Last Game" livelier. Work with students to identify the passive voice. Then suggest ways to recognize passive sentences and ways to replace them with active sentences. You might suggest the following to replace the first sentence: *The fans yelled as soon as the team came onto the court.*
- Have students edit "The Last Game" by changing passive voice to active voice. They may record a class suggestion or write their own paragraph.

Extending the Lesson
During small-group writing instruction, have students select a recent piece of writing from their writing folder that they think needs more active words. Support students as they revise their writing to remove passive voice. Then compare the original and revised versions as a group.

On Your Own
Have students look through other fiction and nonfiction texts to find examples of active voice and words that engage the reader. Encourage students to record some of these in their Writer's Notebook as examples of ways to avoid passive voice.

Assess Progress

Note whether students are able to craft a piece of writing using active voice instead of passive voice. Provide additional practice if necessary.

Writer's Craft — *Keep Language Fresh*

The Last Game

Yelling had been happening since the team came onto the court. Everyone was excited by the last game of the season. Kelly was being cheered by her best friend, Justine. A purple and green flag was being waved by Justine. Players were racing up and down the court. Ten points were scored by Kelly in the fourth quarter. The game was won!

Use Active Voice

Rewrite the paragraph using active voice.

Writer's Craft — End Effectively

Finish on a Strong Note

Lesson Background
Effective writing leaves the reader with something interesting to consider. A writer can end a piece of writing by using humor, asking a question, or using a strong ending. This lesson focuses on ending effectively by using humor.

Teaching the Lesson
- Copy and distribute the End Effectively Master on page 62 of this guide. You may wish to make a transparency of this page for use during whole-class instruction.
- Read the selection "Joining the Circus" aloud as students follow along.
- After reading, discuss the selection with students. *What is the topic of this selection?* (the circus) *What part of the selection is funny?* (the ending) *How did the writer end the selection?* (with a joke)
- Tell students that an effective ending is important because it makes the piece satisfying to read. One way a writer can satisfy readers is to end a piece of writing on a humorous note. As a class, think of things that are funny about a circus. Then ask students to think of other ways to end "Joining the Circus" using humor. You might wish to suggest the following: *Clowns are funny at the circus. We could end the piece by telling a joke about clowns.*
- Have students edit "Joining the Circus" to include a different humorous ending. They may record a class suggestion or write a new humorous ending of their own.

Extending the Lesson
During small-group writing instruction, have students select a recent piece of writing from their writing folder that they think needs a humorous ending. Support students as they revise their writing. Then compare the original and revised versions as a group.

On Your Own
Have students look through other fiction and nonfiction texts to find humorous endings that entertain and satisfy the reader. Encourage students to record some of these in their Writer's Notebook as examples of effective endings.

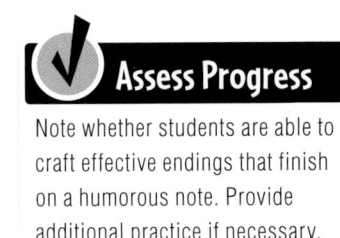

Assess Progress

Note whether students are able to craft effective endings that finish on a humorous note. Provide additional practice if necessary.

Writer's Craft — *End Effectively* **61**

Joining the Circus

I often hear people say that they'd like to run away and join the circus to get away from day-to-day life. I am lucky. I get to be there every day! I have always loved the circus. I am training to be an acrobat. I work three hours each day after school, learning to tumble, flip, roll, and even fall! My brothers and sister are also part of the circus. One of my brothers is a fire-eater, but he really just pretends to eat fire. My other brother and sister are acrobats like me. My dad is a clown! When we are too noisy at home, my mom sometimes says, "I'm going to run away and join the audience!"

Write a Humorous Ending

Write your own humorous ending to "Joining the Circus."

_____
_____
_____
_____
_____
_____
_____

Writer's Craft — Adapt to Purpose and Audience

Aim at the Right Target

Lesson Background
A piece of writing should always have a purpose and a target audience. Writers adapt their language, ideas, and examples for particular purposes and audiences. This lesson focuses on adapting to your purpose by choosing appropriate examples.

Teaching the Lesson
- Copy and distribute the Adapt to Purpose and Audience Master on page 64 of this guide. You may wish to make a transparency of this page for use during whole-class instruction.
- Read the selection "Preparing to Fly" aloud as students follow along.
- After reading, discuss the selection with students. *What is the topic of this selection?* (preparing to fly an airplane) *What is the purpose of this selection?* (to inform the reader about what it is like to fly in a small, private plane) *For whom do you think the selection was written?* (someone who has never been in a small plane) *Are there any details that don't match the purpose?* (Yes, some of the words are not known by the audience.)
- Tell students that good writers decide on their topic and audience and then choose details that will help their readers understand the topic. As a class, decide the author's purpose for writing "Preparing to Fly." Then brainstorm some examples that better match the intended audience and purpose. You might wish to suggest the following: *Describing the roar of the engine and the conversation between the pilot and the control tower would better match the audience and purpose.*
- Have students edit "Preparing to Fly" by rewriting sentences that do not match the purpose and audience. They may record a class suggestion or write details of their own.

Extending the Lesson
During small-group writing instruction, have students select a recent piece of writing from their writing folder that they think needs more appropriate examples for the intended purpose and audience. Support students as they revise their writing. Then compare the original and revised versions as a group.

On Your Own
Have students look through other fiction and nonfiction texts to find examples of a clear purpose and audience. Encourage students to record some of these in their Writer's Notebook as examples of ways to present an understanding of purpose and audience in their own writing.

 **Assess Progress**

Note whether students are able to adapt to purpose and audience by using appropriate examples in their writing. Provide additional practice if necessary.

Preparing to Fly

Flying in a small, private plane is very exciting. You will wear a headset and sit up front in the cockpit. There is not much space in the cockpit, so you will probably be squeezed against other people. You don't have to just sit in the back and read a book like you would on a big plane. You can watch the pilot start the engine, adjust the wing flaps, and begin the takeoff. The fuselage of a plane is usually controlled by the vertical stabilizer and rudder. The vertical and horizontal stabilizers keep the plane level once it is in the air.

Find Your Audience and Purpose

Rewrite sentences that do not match the purpose and audience of this selection.

_____
_____
_____
_____
_____
_____
_____

Name _____ Date _____

Editing Checklist

☐ My name is on my writing piece.

☐ My writing piece has a title.

☐ I read over my piece twice.

☐ I had a friend edit my piece.

☐ My piece is organized and understandable.

☐ I used transitions to connect my words.

☐ I indented my paragraphs.

☐ I checked my grammar.

☐ All of the words are spelled correctly.

☐ I capitalized the first letter of each sentence.

☐ I capitalized all proper nouns.

☐ Each sentence ends with a period, a question mark, or an exclamation point.

☐ I used quotation marks around sentences where someone is speaking.

☐ I used apostrophes to show possession.

☐ This is my best work.

Editing Checklist

Name _____ Date _____

Writer's Reflection Checklist

☐ Title of my writing piece: _____

☐ My favorite part of this piece and why:

_____
_____
_____

☐ What I did to improve my piece was:

_____
_____

☐ What I'm proud of in my writing:

_____
_____

☐ Area I'd like to improve in my writing:

_____
_____

☐ One new idea I have learned about being a writer:

_____
_____

Name_____ Date _____

Writing Traits Checklist

Ideas

- [ ] I have a clear message or story.
- [ ] I used important, interesting details to support my writing.
- [ ] I expressed my ideas in an original way.

Organization

- [ ] I have a strong beginning and ending.
- [ ] There is a title on my work.
- [ ] I put my ideas in an order that makes sense.
- [ ] I used transition words to create links between ideas.

Voice

- [ ] My writing expresses my personality and feelings.
- [ ] My point of view is clear.
- [ ] I wrote in a style that fits my audience.

Word Choice

- [ ] I used strong verbs to show action.
- [ ] I used precise nouns.
- [ ] I used descriptive words that paint a picture for the reader.
- [ ] I used exact words.

Sentence Fluency

- [ ] My writing sounds good when read aloud.
- [ ] I used connecting words.
- [ ] I used creative sentence structures.
- [ ] I varied my sentence length.

Conventions

- [ ] I checked my spelling.
- [ ] I used capital letters correctly.
- [ ] I used punctuation marks correctly.
- [ ] I checked for verb and pronoun correctness.
- [ ] I indented my paragraphs.

Presentation

- [ ] My writing is neat and clear.
- [ ] I used the correct margins.
- [ ] I used pictures, charts, or other visuals to add interest.
- [ ] I added a title.
- [ ] I added headings or page numbers where needed.

Name _____ Date _____

Writer's Craft Checklist

☐ My beginning is effective and makes the audience want to continue reading.

☐ My message is clear and aimed at my audience.

☐ I have included enough information and details.

☐ The reader can hear my "voice" in this piece.

☐ I varied my sentence structure.

☐ The sentences in my piece do not all begin with the same word.

☐ I used active voice.

☐ I organized my thoughts so my piece is easy to follow.

☐ I edited my piece.

☐ My piece could easily be read aloud by another person.

☐ I used exciting words that will interest my audience.

☐ My piece stays on the topic I started with.

☐ I wrote an effective ending.